checklists
for project
managers

checklists for project managers

Your shortcut to success

Richard Newton

Prentice Hall
is an imprint of

Harlow, England • London • New York • Boston • San Francisco • Toronto
Sydney • Tokyo • Singapore • Hong Kong • Seoul • Taipei • New Delhi
Cape Town • Madrid • Mexico City • Amsterdam • Munich • Paris • Milan

PEARSON EDUCATION LIMITED
Edinburgh Gate
Harlow CM20 2JE
Tel: +44(0)1279 623623
Fax: +44(0)1279 431059
Website: www.pearsoned.co.uk

First published 2008 (published as *The Project Manager's Book of Checklists*)
Second edition 2011

ISBN: 978-0-273-74076-6

British Library Cataloguing-in-Publication Data
A catalogue record for this book is available from the British Library

Library of Congress Cataloging-in-Publication Data
Newton, Richard, 1964-
    Brilliant checklists for project managers : your shortcut to success
/   Richard Newton. -- 2nd ed.
        p. cm.
    Rev. ed. of: The project manager's book of checklists : everything
you need to complete a project successfully, smoothly, and on time.
2008.
    ISBN 978-0-273-74076-6 (pbk.)
  1.   Project management.   I.   Newton, Richard, 1964- Project manager's
book of checklists.   II.   Title.
    HD69.P75N497 2010
    658.4'04--dc22

                                                          2010036275

10 9 8 7 6 5 4 3 2 1
14 13 12 11 10

Typeset in 10.5pt/11.5pt Plantin by 30
Printed by Ashford Colour Press Ltd, Gosport, Hants

This book is dedicated to Ike and Amy Newton

About the author

Richard Newton is a delivery manager, author and management consultant. He helps organisations develop sustainable capabilities to deliver projects and change. He specialises in shaping, mobilising and delivering complex programmes.

Richard splits his time between running change initiatives, managing his consulting company Enixus, writing, and public speaking. He has over 25 years of business experience in a wide variety of organisations.

Richard is the author of seven books, which have been translated into over a dozen languages. He works internationally, but when at home lives in the Cotswolds, UK. Outside of work, he enjoys walking in wild, mountainous and remote places.

Contents

Introduction

T his book provides a comprehensive source of hints, tips and guidance to help you finish tasks at work. It starts by considering straightforward tasks you do on your own, moves through working as a team, and then enters the world of projects.

The book is structured to flick through the contents list and go straight to the checklist you want. If you are not sure which individual checklist will solve your immediate problem you can use the book in a hierarchical fashion. Start at the checklist below and work down to the detailed advice you need. In most cases it is obvious which specific checklist you need. But where the chapter you have been pointed to is complex, it also starts with an introductory checklist or advice to help you navigate.

The checklists have a variety of formats. Many are lists of advice, some are tables, and others are template forms. Where bullet points are used, the order of the points is not important. In contrast, where numbered points are used the checklist provides a roughly logical procedure – although common sense needs to be applied.

There are links between checklists to help you navigate between different chapters. The best way to use the book is to simply dive in. Why not read through the checklist below? It points to wherever you need to go.

Whatever journey you need to make to get the task done, this book will help you get there.

Which checklist do you need?

- You are working alone and want some simple advice on making your time more productive . . . *go to Chapter 1.*

- You are working with a small team and need help in ensuring the team does what you want them to do . . . *go to Chapter 2.*

- You know you want something done but you are having trouble getting your ideas clear . . . *go to Chapters 3 and 4.*

- You want a project(s) accepted and approved by others in your organisation . . . *refer to the checklists in Chapter 4, and see the checklist on page 189.*

- You want to make a project concept clearer . . . *go to Chapter 5.*

- Your project is understood and approved. Now you just need to get started . . . *go to Chapter 6.*

- You need advice on how to keep your project running smoothly and successfully . . . *refer to the checklists in Chapter 7, see page 144, and then look at Chapter 10.*

- Your want to finish your project in the best possible way . . . *go to Chapter 8, and then try Chapters 13 and 14.*

- Your project is now over and you want to make sure that the things you have learnt are captured . . . *go to Chapter 9.*

- You want to understand and make use of the full range of tools available to project managers . . . *start with the checklists on pages 61 and 144 and then go to Chapter 10.*

- You have several projects or a programme to run and want to make sure you can keep on top of them . . . *refer to the checklists in Chapter 11, and try the checklist on page 172.*

- You want to set up or are already managing a team of project managers . . . *refer to the checklists in Chapter 12, and then try see pages 82, 94, 144 and 183.*

- Your project will result in business or organisational change . . . *go to Chapter 13.*

- You have business benefits to achieve with your project . . . *go to Chapter 14.*

- You need to set up and manage a project budget . . . *see pages 72, 89, 168 and 235.*

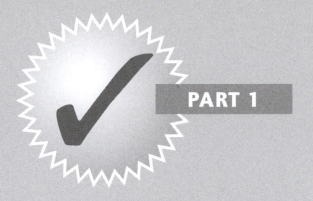

PART 1

Managing straightforward tasks

This part helps you manage simple tasks performed by you or your team. There are three chapters in this section:

1 **Personal work management** – managing your own time and work.

2 **Managing others' activity** – overseeing other people and their work.

3 **Clarifying problems and opportunities** – making sure ideas are sufficiently understood.

Every activity, project and even the largest programme relies on individuals knowing what they need to do and managing their own time to get it done. The foundations of all successful projects are well-disciplined project team members.

CHAPTER 1

Personal work management

This chapter helps you to control your workload better. It assumes you are a member of a team with a line manager, and want some advice on making your own time more productive.

Understanding your workload

To manage your time you must understand your workload. Projects will always be a struggle if you cannot plan your own time. The following table provides a tool to plan your time better. It is a tool to be used quickly. Don't over-analyse the questions! Rough estimates will do.

		Hours	Total hours
How many hours per week do you expect to work?			
		A	_____
How much time do you spend on personal administration and basic everyday tasks?	What are these tasks? How much time do you spend on them? For example: ● completing standard administration ● completing unavoidable communications (emails, phone calls, etc.) ● meetings you must attend or appointments (check your diary) ● giving help to other people ● coffee bar chats, etc.		
	B.1	_____	
Do you have a series of team management activities?	What are the activities? How much time do you spend on them? For example: ● allocating work ● checking work ● performance reviews ● budget management ● reporting, etc.		
	B.2	_____	

→

		Hours	Total hours
Do you have a series of other regular tasks to do on a daily basis?	What are the activities? How much time do they take?		
	B.3	_____	
Do you have a series of additional regular tasks to do on a weekly basis?	What are the activities? How much time do they take?		
	B.4	_____	
Are there any other periodic tasks you have to do?	What are they? How much time do they take in an average week?		
	B.5	_____	
Do you often get adhoc or one-off tasks to do?	How much time per week do they typically take?		
	B.6	_____	
	Total hours used per week: $B = B.1 + B.2 + B.3 + B.4 + B.5 + B.6$		
	B		_____
	Normal available hours $C = A - B$		
	C		_____
Do you have any peaks in workload at specific times of the month or year?	How many hours do these add to your work?		
	E		_____
	Peak available hours $F = C - E$		
	F		_____

The important numbers are C and F:

- C is the time you have for additional work *including projects*.

- If C is negative then you need to become more efficient or reduce the amount you are doing. The checklists on pages 8–20 will help.

- The same applies to F for peak periods of the year. If F is a positive number you have time for more work, including projects. F will probably be negative. This is not necessarily a problem, depending on how long and frequent your peaks are.

Writing an effective action list to plan your work

High productivity starts with self-management. Often, you will have more to do than can be done in the available time. This means making choices about what you do and how long you spend on each activity. Follow these tips, but it is *your* action list so make them work for you:

1 Choose a time period for your action list – is it a day or a week? Don't plan for too short a period: generally, planning for less than a day is not productive. Action lists are simple tools and are not that useful for long periods (other than as memory joggers).

2 Write down the tasks you need to complete in the time period you have chosen.

3 Choose a practical level of detail. The action list is to help you plan your day. It does not need detailed instructions for every task, nor should it be at such a high level that you cannot work out a proper order.

4 Group tasks which are efficient to do at the same time – e.g., if one of your tasks is to put a new exhaust on your car, and another is to get new tyres, do them at the same time!

5 Put the tasks into priority order (see page 10).

6 Add in extra time for:

   ● Your normal mandatory day-to-day work (if you did not include it in point 2).

   ● Unexpected tasks or interruptions.

   ● Seeking help and advice on tasks you must do, but don't know how to.

   ● Coffee breaks, relaxation, etc. No one can work flat out 100 per cent of the time. Use common sense in determining how much.

7 Remove tasks you are never going to be able to do:

   ● Delete optional unnecessary tasks. If it helps, keep a separate list of activities you may do in the future when you have the capacity. It is important to keep these separate from your main action list.

   ● Delegate other work where possible and appropriate.

8 Advise your line manager if there are essential tasks you will not have time to complete.

9 Check: if you look through the list of activities you have written down – does it represent what your job is meant to be? Will you achieve your objectives if you continue to do tasks like this?

10 Check your diary: is there enough time to do this? Set aside time in your diary to complete your task list. This is helpful if there are important tasks that never get done because of interruptions or urgent things that get in the way. Put an appointment for yourself in your diary to do important work.

Prioritising your workload

When there are too many things to do we have to prioritise them. Prioritisation is an essential part of work, but it is usually hard to do as it requires us to make difficult choices.

1   Determine the basis for prioritising your work – what criteria will you use to decide what task to do first?

   ● Start by thinking about: what task adds the most value and what tasks are least important? Why do you think this – what rule are you applying to determine this? In your role, what are the core goals you have to achieve?

2   Make sure you understand the difference between *urgent* and *important*. Don't simply put all the urgent tasks as the first you will do.

3   Remove tasks that you know you will never have time to do and should not be doing.

4   Decide what is the most important activity on your work list. If you could only do one thing what would it be? This is your highest-priority task.

5   Check that your choice is consistent with your prioritisation criteria.

6   If you could only do one more task, what would it be? Keep doing this until you have everything in order.

7   See if all the meetings in your diary are a priority. Meetings may be important, but don't have meetings just because they are in the diary as a regular event. Meetings have to be prioritised too. Don't feel afraid to say no to them.

8   Compare your list with the time you have to work on it. If there is more to do than you have time for, remove non-value-adding tasks (see page 11), ask your line manager for some help (see page 15), or delegate work (see page 18).

Key tips for prioritising your work:

● Practise prioritising regularly. At first it will take time, but with practice it should only take a few minutes every day.

● Start every day by reviewing your work and deciding what's the highest priority, and what you aim to complete in that day.

● Don't leave hard, unpleasant or uncertain tasks until last! Do them early, so if they take more time than expected you can still complete them.

● Base prioritisation on your objectives. If you don't have objectives or they are not clear, talk to your line manager or boss and ask for guidance.

Removing non-value-adding tasks from your work

Typically, we do many things we don't need to. They may be things we like doing or have never questioned. The effect is to stop us doing more valuable tasks. Productive people are good at minimising the non-value-adding parts of their work.

For any of the questions you answer yes – try to reduce or eliminate corresponding activity from your work.

Symptoms of non-value-adding task	Yes	Constructively reduce your workload by . . .
Is there anything you do that no one seems to benefit from?	☐	Stop doing it! (You'll soon find out if it really was needed or not!)
Do you frequently answer emails, text messages, instant messages and so on?	☐	Don't answer them the second they arrive. Ignore and delete any that are junk. Answer the others between more important tasks. Set aside fixed times in the day to handle email. Avoid constantly stopping work for emails or similar interruptions.
Do you often get telephone calls?	☐	The phone can be ignored and left to go to answer-phone to be handled later.
Do you often deal with unwanted visitors who you can avoid?	☐	Explain you are busy. Ask people to arrange times to see you. Where you can't avoid the interruption, politely make clear you are short of time and need to talk quickly.
Do you have many other interruptions to your work?	☐	If you are constantly interrupted the amount of work you complete will decline. Set rules for when you can be interrupted. Cut yourself off physically – work in a closed-off office or at home.

→

Symptoms of non-value-adding task	Yes	Constructively reduce your workload by . . .
Do you spend a significant proportion of your time sorting out work or arranging papers?	☐	Sorting work helps you to be efficient, but it should not take long. If you are doing too much – stop it!
Do you spend an unreasonable amount of time planning, as opposed to actioning, your work?	☐	Keep planning short. Planning is essential and it makes you more efficient and effective. But you get rewarded for doing, not planning.
Do you spend too much time doing low-priority work, when there are higher-priority activities you should do first?	☐	Plan out your work, and start with the highest-priority work first.
Are you often interrupted to do urgent as opposed to important work?	☐	Do the important work first. If you cannot avoid urgent tasks, set aside a slot at the beginning or end of the day for them.
Do you often do other people favours when you should really be saying no to them?	☐	Sometimes say no. If you can't do this, go on an assertiveness training course.
Are you unwilling to delegate because you think you do it best?	☐	Trust the person and delegate. If you never delegate they won't learn to do it. Every time you don't delegate you are choosing not to do other work you should be doing.
Do you spend much of your time solving other people's problems, or doing other people's work?	☐	Try to support your colleagues, but not at the cost of your own workload.
Do you often find yourself having to redo work that has been done wrongly or to insufficient quality?	☐	Redoing work is a waste of time. Avoid it by understanding the requirements up front – including the level of quality required.
Do you spend a lot of time at work in social chit-chat or coffee bar conversations?	☐	Monitor yourself. We need interaction, and some issues can be resolved by a quick chat. If your chats are turning into regular 30-minute sessions, reduce them.

Symptoms of non-value-adding task	Yes	Constructively reduce your workload by ...
Do you spend significant amounts of time in unproductive meetings?	☐	Only go to meetings with a specific objective and an agenda. (Make sure this applies to your meetings too!)
Do you spend significant amounts of time in travelling between locations?	☐	Travel time is wasted time. Many face-to-face meetings are unnecessary. Try conference calls, or a videoconference.
Do you spend lots of time perfecting work that really does not need polishing?	☐	Stop! The quality of the content counts, not how neat or pretty it is.
Is there a better or more efficient way to do any of the activities you need to do?	☐	Think, research, ask a more experienced colleague. Every day, try and do one thing better.
Are you wasting time by always swapping between tasks without completing anything?	☐	Plan, prioritise and complete. There's no reward for starting lots of tasks, only for completing them.

Working to an action list

Have you ever written an action list and later found you never used it?

1   Use it – don't just write it and forget it.

2   Work in the priority order.

3   Avoid the temptation to jump to the easiest tasks all the time. We all need to give ourselves a pat on the back, and ticking off a few easy tasks now and again does no harm – but don't spend any more than a small percentage of your time doing this.

4   Remember: the action list is only guidance and not a straitjacket. Be willing to change it if the situation changes.

5   Maintain the action list. When you created it, it was your understanding of what needed doing then – your understanding changes quickly. Every morning take a few minutes to reflect and maintain your action list.

6   Watch out for the ever-increasing list – it's a sign that you are out of control.

7   Complete tasks. Don't just start everything. Only tick something off once it is really completed.

8   Complete tasks to the appropriate level of quality. Avoid shortcuts by doing work poorly, but also avoid perfecting everything. There is an appropriate level of quality for every task. Any time you overdo it you are choosing to spend less time on something else.

9   If a task is always at the bottom of the list and is never going to be done, strike it off. If it must be done, get some help. Hints:

   ● If you don't want to lose sight of the task, create a separate list of things you want to remember, but don't have the time to do. Make sure this is separate from your action list.

   ● If you have gaps in your day fit in the small tasks. Those 10 minutes before you leave or go to lunch can tick off half a dozen emails or a couple of calls.

10 Keep control of interruptions and other non-value-adding tasks.

Deciding when you need help

Everyone needs help sometimes, but it can be awkward to ask. Successful people know when to get help. Whether it is asking for a hint, or asking someone to take on part of your work – *help helps*!

There are several telltale signs that you need help. For any of the following questions you answer yes to, look to get some help.

Can you carry on alone or do you need help?	Yes	Consider the following
Do you ever find you don't know what you should be doing?	☐	Ask your line manager to define what he or she wants you to do in sufficient detail for you to understand. If you cannot ask your line manager, try asking a colleague who does a similar job.
Do you fail to get everything done you think you should be doing?	☐	Focus and prioritise. Continue working through this list.
Are you unsure how to prioritise your work?	☐	See page 10.
Do you fail to complete all your priority work?	☐	Get help or get more productive. Use this checklist to get help, or develop a plan to enhance your skills.
Have you reviewed all the things you do – are any unnecessary?	☐	Remove non-essential tasks. See page 11.
Is your task list continually lengthening?	☐	Cut down the work or get help to complete it.
Is this normal, or is it just a blip?	☐	If it's just a blip then a little push or overtime will help.
If you did one or a few stints of overtime would you reduce your task list to an achievable length?	☐	A few days to remove a backlog is worthwhile, but don't get into the habit of it.
Are you regularly taking work home?	☐	Unless your job really is your vocation, stop! Focus, prioritise, and seek help.

→

Can you carry on alone or do you need help?	Yes	Consider the following
At your present rate of work, and if work continues to be added at the same rate, will your task list continue to expand?	☐	Do something now! Review your action list and prioritise your work effectively. Work out how much you can do. Set up a discussion with your line manager once you have reviewed your action list.
Are there any unnecessary or optional tasks on your list that you can drop?	☐	See page 11.
Do you lack any skills or competency to do everything you are meant to do?	☐	Talk to your line manager and ask for the relevant training (see page 18).
Is there any way you can expand your capacity to work?	☐	Think about better planning, prioritisation, more delegation, skills training, or tools. Ask an experienced colleague for advice.
Are you always bogged down in fixing urgent issues rather than working on the more important things?	☐	Prioritise more effectively (see page 10).
Are you the only person who seems to know how to do something?	☐	Train up someone else – the effort will be worth it in the longer run.
Do you constantly have to answer questions from colleagues and team members beyond what seems reasonable?	☐	Say no (see page 20).
Are you doing any work you do not have the necessary permissions or authority to do?	☐	Say no to it (see page 20).
Are you doing any work you feel you should not be doing?	☐	Ensure your feeling is reasonable. If it is, say no (see page 20).
Are you doing any work you do not have the proper tools or facilities to do?	☐	Ask for the tools or facilities. If the right tools are not available say no to the task (see page 20). Offer to help defining the tools needed and in developing them.

Can you carry on alone or do you need help?	Yes	Consider the following
Are you involved in any activities that you do not need to be? (You have nothing to add and it adds nothing to your work.)	☐	Stop!
Do you find you never have time to think and plan, but always get swamped by immediate tasks?	☐	Start every day planning your day. End every week by planning the next week. Effective thinking and planning will more than save the time you spend doing it.

Getting your line manager's support

Your line manager is also responsible for ensuring you can do your work. Line managers won't automatically know if you have problems, and you may need to ask them for help.

1   Before you ask for support, check with yourself that the request is reasonable.

2   Be clear about what help you need and why you need it. Think through what precisely you will ask for when you see your line manager.

3   Try to make it worth his or her while to help you . . . *I have a problem, but if you can help me solve it then I will be able to do this better in future . . . If you let me go on this training course I could do this for you*, etc.

4   Help your line manager to help you. Express your need in a way you know they will understand. Just because she is the line manager does not mean she is the expert in your field!

5   If you can offer solutions as well as difficulties . . . *I can't do this, but if you let me . . . I could.*

6   Remember you are asking for help, not trying to get out of work. Don't make it sound or look as if you are simply avoiding work.

7   If you are stuck, don't avoid asking team members, colleagues or line managers. When you ask for help – ask if it's OK to come back with further questions.

8   When you have been helped, always thank the person. You want to build a good relationship with anyone who is willing to help you.

Delegating activities

When your workload is too big you must delegate part to someone else. If you need help in finding out to whom you can allocate work, talk to your line manager.

To delegate, think about:

1 Why are you delegating (it's not your role, you don't have time, you want them to learn how to do it)? Be willing to explain this to the person you delegate to.

2 Ask yourself – is it reasonable to delegate this work?

3 Make sure you understand the task you are delegating and that you can explain it. (See page 25.)

4 How much freedom will you give the person you delegate to? (Do they have to do it as you want or can they explore other ways? Do you actively want them to find out?) (See page 25.)

5 Can you simply explain the outcome you want, or do you need to explain the steps in doing it? Try to do the former unless you must do the latter.

6 Identify the person who will do it. Do they have the skills and competencies? What help will they need from you?

7 Explain the importance and urgency of the work. Are you being reasonable?

8 Check they have the time to do the task.

9 Help them prioritise this task versus their other work.

10 Tell them what success in this task looks like. What level of quality is required?

11 Be clear how you will monitor progress.

12 Give the person you are delegating to any tips or advice before they start.

When and how to say no to a task

If you never say no, you will always be overloaded. Saying no for the right reasons is the right thing to do. When you accept a task, you choose not to use the time to do something else. Help yourself by saying no. Say no when:

- You have too much to do and you are willing to accept the implications of saying no – or think you can manage your way around them.
- You don't have the skills or competency to do the task, and getting it wrong will have serious implications for your organisation.
- There is someone else who can do it who is not busy and you can identify them.
- There is someone else who has offered to do it and who has the right skills.
- There is someone else who can do it and you will help them to do it.
- It will have a negative impact on your lifestyle beyond what you can put up with.
- You have to give up something else you really want to do at work.

Having decided you are not going to do a task you must decide how you are going to say no. You need to be assertive, not aggressive, when saying no. It is possible to reject a task in a positive way. Some tips are:

- Is the task pointless or avoidable? Tell the requester, nicely.
- Can you simply refuse to do it without fear of repercussion? Then do!
- Are you clear in your own mind why you don't want to do it? Is this reasonable? Base your rejection of the task around this.
- Do you understand why the task is important? If not, check before you reject it.
- Does the requester understand the implications if you do the task? Someone may not understand why you cannot do it: explain without making it sound like an excuse.
- Can you give the requester options for how else to do it? This is helpful and positive.
- Can you understand the requester's viewpoint? If you can, this makes it easier to explain in a sympathetic way why you cannot do it.

brilliant   **recap**

Effective people regularly review what is needed and prioritise their efforts on the most important and value-adding tasks. They don't approach their work in a haphazard manner. They are not afraid to ignore less-critical activities, even if they seem urgent.

CHAPTER 2

Managing others' activity

This chapter contains checklists to manage others' work. Project success depends on the project manager's ability to direct the project team members to do the project activities.

Defining tasks and setting objectives for others

The starting point for getting anyone else to do a task is to define what you want. This checklist contains key points to consider when defining a task.

1   Define the nature of the task. Think how you like things explained to you. You should be able to answer the following questions before you try to explain it to others:

- What is the task?
- Why does this task need to be done?
- How important is the task? What priority is it?
- What are the constraints on doing it (is there a time limit, can anyone else be asked for help, is there a budget, etc.)?
- Can the task be done in any way, or must it follow a defined process or be done in a specific way?
- How will you judge whether it has been successfully completed or not?
- Are there any expectations or requirements about the outcome that need to be spelled out?
- Are there any rewards for doing the task?

2   Having defined the task, check understanding by asking the person doing it to describe back to you what they should be doing. Correct any mistakes in their understanding.

3   Agree when you will get back together.

- If it is a simple task that the person doing it is familiar with, then you don't need to see them until they have completed it.
- If the task is more complex, or is of a type that the person doing is unfamiliar with, agree times for checkpoints to assess progress and ensure the outcome will meet your needs. (See page 30.)

brilliant   tip

In asking someone to do a task you can prescriptively define how it is to be done, or you can give leeway to interpret what is required. Generally, it is good to be less prescriptive and to be open to an individual's creativity. This often results in a better solution and enables the individual to develop. Being continuously prescriptive indicates you either have poor management skills or have the wrong team!

There are no hard rules, and the following table lists factors to consider in making a decision about how prescriptive to be.

Be more prescriptive if . . .	Give more freedom if . . .
● The task has to be done in a specific way due to legal, regulatory, health and safety or other rules. ● The person doing the task has no expertise in this type of task or anything similar. ● There is a time or cost limit which will be better fulfilled by being prescriptive. ● No help is available when doing the task, and it is critical that it be done correctly. ● You do not trust the person doing the work.	● You want a creative or novel solution. ● You do not know how to do it. ● The person doing the task has greater expertise than you. ● It is important for the person doing the task to develop. ● There is help, support or regular feedback available. ● It is fair and reasonable to expect the person to be able to work it out for themselves. ● The task is non-critical. ● There is insufficient time to explain the outcome or process.

Understanding skills and resources needed for a task

What skills or knowledge are required?

- What technical or specialist knowledge is needed?
- Are formal qualifications required – is this a task that must be done by someone who has a recognised accreditation?
- Is this a task one person can do on their own, or does it require interacting with many others? If so, what interpersonal skills are needed?
- Does the task need any management skills?
- Is position or power important to completing this task?
- Is the ability to be creative helpful?
- Is knowledge of the business and environment essential or helpful – or is it better if the person doing the work is free from preconceived ideas?
- Is any other task-specific skill or knowledge needed?

What human resources are required?

- How big or complex is the task?
- How much time is available to complete the task?
- How quickly is it required?
- Can it be broken down into pieces? How? As a result, how many people could work on this in parallel?
- Can any of the work be outsourced or contracted out? Do you have a budget for this?

Other resources required?

- What other resources are required (e.g., consumables, infrastructure, facilities, tools, IT systems, etc.).
- Are these available? If not, can you source them?

Choosing the right person to do a task

Being successful in projects is not just about allocating work to team members, it's also about choosing the right person for each task. Factors in choosing the right person to do the work are:

1   Is there a choice of person? If there is:
    - Who has the most capacity to do the work?
    - Who is the most reliable person with this type of work?
    - What are the levels of motivation among the available people?
    - Who has the skills or knowledge to do the work?
    - Is it more important to get the task done right or quickly?
    - Is it important to expand the skills in a business, department or team, or reduce dependency on scarce resources?

2   What support is needed, and how does this affect the choice of person?
    - How much time or help from you or another skilled professional is available to support this task?
    - How much time do you have available to oversee or manage the task?
    - How much help or support will the different people who could do the task need?

3   What is the impact and what is your contingency plan should the person chosen fail to complete the work to the necessary level of quality?
    - How likely is it that the person chosen will not do the work, or will do it incorrectly?
    - Can you regularly check progress to decrease this likelihood?
    - Who could take over or help deliver the task, if necessary?

Checking progress

Keeping track of progress gives confidence that work is being done on time, and provides the opportunity to assist the person doing the work. The following table provides guidance on how to check progress and how often.

Issue	Implications for progress checking
Has the person doing the task fed back a clear understanding of what you require, and agreed to do this?	Get this understanding and agreement. If not possible, have more, regular progress checks.
Have you agreed when you will meet to assess progress?	As part of task definition, agree when you will review progress and what you expect to see.
Are you happy with the approach and outcome the person doing the work is proposing?	If not, make clear what changes you expect.
Is the task fully defined, or are you expecting some creativity or exploration of options as part of the work?	If you require the use of initiative, plan early checkpoints, when there is enough time to adapt if what is being done is not what is wanted.
How do you assess progress with this task?	Ensure you have a way of understanding what progress is being made.
Is the person an expert with greater knowledge than you?	Fewer, shorter checkpoints are required. If you are the expert, ensure you have time to provide help and support.
Do you lack confidence in the person's ability or motivation to complete the task?	Plan early checkpoints, when there is enough time to adapt if what is being done is not what is wanted.
Have you agreed when you will *next* meet to discuss progress?	Always agree when you will meet next. If the person's work did not meet expectations, meet again soon.

Helping someone else to complete a task

With delegation comes a responsibility to provide help and support. Tips to providing help are:

- Be open to requests for help. It's you who needs the task done, and it's you who will suffer if it's done badly.

- Listen to the request. Make sure you really understand what help is needed, and don't jump to conclusions as to what to do.

- Try to get the requester to ask specific questions. It's far easier to answer a specific question, even if it is as big as '*I don't know how to get started*'.

- Try not to do the work for them. Help them to work out what they need to do rather than do it for them. Ask questions like '*What could be a better way?*' or '*Can you see an alternative approach?*' rather than tell them how to do it.

- From time to time offer support without being asked. People remember team members and managers who actively support them, and you will get better results.

- If they really can't understand, and time is pressing – get someone else to do the work. But only do this if you must! Remember: doing this often is a management failure as you chose the wrong person, and did not help them to develop.

Managing tasks across a team

Sometimes tasks are best done by several people. This can speed delivery times but can make the management of the task a little more complex. If the task is being split:

- Ensure it makes sense to break the tasks into different pieces (some work cannot be broken down).

- Clarify who you are expecting to do what. If you want the team to decompose the task into different pieces themselves, make this clear.

- Ensure there are no gaps and overlaps between the activities the task is broken into.

- If you think the team members will not work constructively together, make one person a team leader responsible for resolving disputes.

- Ensure it is clear who pulls the different pieces of work together into one final deliverable. Although the work is broken down you will usually want one output, not several.

- Clarify when and how you would like the team to come to you for review, feedback or to escalate any problems that arise which the team cannot resolve.

Getting someone to do a task when you aren't their line manager

This is a common challenge for project managers. Factors to consider when getting someone, who does not work for you, to do a task:

- Ask nicely! Don't treat every request as a confrontation. Use your influencing skills. Asking for support in the right way makes it more likely that you will get the help you need.

- Ask confidently and don't appear apologetic. It is quite reasonable to ask people to do work for you. It is their responsibility to say no if they cannot.

- Choose the time to ask. There are times when it's far easier to get help than not. For example, asking an accountant for help at month-end is less likely to get a positive response than asking in the middle of the month.

- Don't accept the first no. Always try a little persuasion.

- Be willing to negotiate. If the person does this task, show what the benefit for them is. This does not have to be a reward, but can be something trivial such as '*I will be really pleased*', '*You will have the opportunity to impress the sponsor*', etc.

- Explain the importance of the work. Most people are reasonable and will help out with important tasks.

- See if there is something you can do for them in return. This can be small, but important to them. '*If you do this, I'll make sure the boss knows what a great help you've been*'.

- If possible, ask their line manager for support. '*I want to get x to do y – can you support me?*'

- Escalate to your project sponsor if you are getting nowhere, but don't do this too often. (See page 115.)

- If you struggle to get others to do work for you, find someone you know who always manages to get things done by other people. What do they do that you don't?

And when someone has done some work for you well, remember to thank them. Saying thanks goes a long way, and you may be asking them for help again soon!

brilliant **recap**

All projects, even the largest and most complex, depend on individuals completing their assigned activities. The fundamental management skills in any situation are the abilities to select the most appropriate people, to define tasks and set objectives, and to monitor progress and provide appropriate help.

CHAPTER 3

Clarifying problems and opportunities

Projects are often initiated to explore
and implement solutions to problems,
or to take advantage of opportunities.
Effective projects need a definition of
the problem they are setting out to
solve, the solution they are trying to
implement, or the opportunity they
want to seize.

Identifying problems and opportunities

There are many ways to identify current problems and opportunities. Start by listening to suggestions, being alert to what is happening in the organisation, and being willing to change. It is often a vague idea that starts a project rolling. Sources of ideas include:

- Operational management – what issues and problems are arising? What do we do well we should do more of?
- Performance metrics – what are the areas of underperformance, what are the trends? (Trends are always more informative than single pieces of data.)
- Interviews – managers, staff, customers, focus groups, etc. What ideas and concerns do they have?
- Observation – keeping eyes and ears open around the organisation. What are staff, customers and suppliers talking about? Do these conversations contain any good ideas?
- Technology – what new technology is available, and how can we take advantage of it?
- Market research – what is happening in the market and in competing organisations?
- Reviews using techniques such as brainstorming or other idea-generation approaches.
- Suggestion boxes and taking advantage of staff insights.

Organisations should be aware of future problems and opportunities, and managers must regularly ask themselves:

- What changes are taking place in the environment of this organisation?
- What risks is the organisation exposed to? How are risks evolving?
- What are the areas the organisation's performance is most sensitive to (both positive and negative)?
- What technology trends can be identified – do they pose any threat or opportunity?

- What are competitors doing – does this pose any threat or opportunity?
- What are suppliers doing – does this pose any threat or opportunity?
- How are customer needs evolving – does this pose any threat or opportunity?
- How are staff needs and interests evolving – does this pose any threat or opportunity?
- Are you listening to ideas from your staff?
- Are there any other stakeholders whose interests, needs or desires are changing?

Understanding the impact of a problem

Understanding the impact of problems will help in prioritising which problems are resolved and in developing project business cases.

1   How does the problem manifest itself:
    - Who or what is affected by the problem?
    - When or in what conditions are they affected? Is it the whole time, or only at certain times or in certain conditions? If the problem is intermittent, try to identify when it occurs.
    - In what way are they affected by the problem?

2   How can the problem manifestations be measured or, if quantification is not possible, described?

3   Is there a baseline for this measure when the problem is not occurring or before it started? What is the incremental change brought about by the problem?

4   Are you sure which problem is causing what impacts – or are the symptoms a manifestation of the interaction of multiple problems? If so, do you understand the relationship between problems?

5   Are there any workarounds or fixes which enable people to overcome this problem? Can you just accept the problem and use the fixes? If not, why not?

6   What is the potential benefit of resolving the problem?

Root cause analysis

Root cause analysis identifies the originating cause of problems. Problems have many symptoms and it is the symptoms that often become the focus of management attention. Organisations waste huge resources treating the symptoms. It is always more effective to resolve the root cause.

There are several approaches to root cause analysis, including *Ishikawa* or *fishbone diagrams, 5 whys* and *fault tree analysis*. Irrespective of technique used, the basic steps are:

1   Define the problem – root cause analysis works from a clear, succinct definition of the problem that needs to be resolved. It cannot be applied to poorly defined problems.

2   Gather data and evidence – what evidence and metrics exist to show the problem? What information exists on this problem?

3   Identify issues that contribute to the problem – analyse the problem and think through the possible related issues that may have contributed. For each issue ask what happened, and when, how and why it happened.

4   Find root causes:

   ● Structure the issues into a chain of events – linking causes to effects. Start with the 'final' effects.

   ● Identify the causes of each effect by determining why it occurred. Don't confuse effects for causes. This is a common mistake. A cause may link to multiple effects.

   ● If the cause has its own identifiable cause, you have not reached the root cause.

   ● When you cannot sensibly answer why the event occurred you have reached the root cause.

   ● If you find you cannot continue because of a lack of information – return to Step 3.

5   Check the logic in your chain of events:

- Ensure nothing is missed out.
- Eliminate all ideas from the analysis that are not root causes.
- If you used assumptions ensure that this is understood as you could be wrong. Try to verify all assumptions.

6   Resolve the root cause of the problem:

- As you implement your resolution, measure and monitor the problem symptoms (effects) to ensure they disappear.
- If they do not, the wrong root cause has been identified and further work is required – return to Step 2.

Generating opportunities and solutions

The checklists on pages 37–40 will help you to understand the problems you have. Problems are overcome by solutions. Fortunately, life is not just about solving problems – there are also opportunities for improvement. This checklist is written from the viewpoint of a solution to a known problem, but it will also work in identifying new opportunities.

1   Make sure there is a clear understanding of what is wanted. Don't jump too soon to a solution. You are answering a question like 'I want to overcome problem X', not something of the form 'I want to do Y'. For example, 'I want to transport a 250kg box from London to Edinburgh', not 'I want to hire a Ford Transit van'.

2   Document the problem succinctly and unambiguously. If you can't express it in a sentence or two, you won't be able to focus people on working out a solution to it.

3   Challenge yourself and your team, and if appropriate your customers and suppliers, with regard to this problem:

   ● What do your competitors do?

   ● Who really understands this issue?

   ● Are there other organisations who you can talk to, to discuss ideas?

   ● What books, journals, websites, blogs are available on this topic? Who is reading them?

   ● Are there specialists or consultants who can advise you?

   ● Are there other areas we can gain inspiration from?

   ● What is an off-the-wall suggestion?

4   Create an atmosphere in which innovation and creativity thrive. Build expertise, motivation and excitement for creativity, and creative thinking skills. Do not set too tight constraints or limits. Identify and challenge inherent assumptions.

5 Go beyond the obvious. If every idea is obvious, try harder! Recognise and be open to unusual opportunities. The most successful businesses do something different.

6 Set aside time for thinking as an individual or group. Make use of sessions with an expert facilitator, use brainstorming or visioning techniques. Consider investing in a creativity or innovation approach.

7 Define the characteristics of a good solution, but try not to include too many constraints that limit your thinking.

8 For every solution generated, do a comparison to the original problem definition. If you implement this solution, will you really overcome the problem?

Exploring ideas

Solutions or opportunities need to be detailed to be taken forward. A one-line definition is not enough to achieve an outcome. The level of detail required depends on the situation. For a small task there needs to be enough detail for the work to be performed. For a complex situation or project, there needs to be sufficient detail for a project to be scoped, sized and prioritised. For a project you need to have sufficient detail to answer the question: *Is this an idea we want to pursue?*

1   Start with a clear and, if possible, unambiguous definition of the idea:

   ● Clarify ambiguities that can be clarified.

   ● Provide sufficient detail for everyone to understand what the idea is.

   ● If the idea breaks into logical components, describe these – but don't force its decomposition if it is not natural or the decomposition constrains thinking.

2   Balance realism (this idea has to work) with an open mind (it may be improvable). Avoid expanding the scope by adding too many bells and whistles, but do explore the potential of ideas. Remember the idea will be implemented at some stage.

3   Try to improve on the idea:

   ● What assumptions are related to this idea?

   ● Are they realistic and reasonable?

   ● Do any assumptions constrain the idea – can conditions be made in which the assumptions are false?

   ● What combinations or reductions in scope can be made?

   ● Can you combine good bits from other ideas to improve this idea?

   ● Can you subtract or remove parts to make it more attractive or practical?

   ● Are there any aspects of the idea you can magnify or reduce to improve it?

   ● Can you rearrange the idea in any way to make it better?

   ● Can you substitute parts of the idea with other ideas or existing solutions?

   ● What other modifications or adaptations can you make to the idea?

4   Keep asking *why* and therefore *what* and *how*. Expand and detail the idea.

Choosing between solutions

You cannot implement everything. You have to whittle down lots of ideas to a set of concepts that you have the resources to implement.

1   Be clear about the problem the solutions are designed to resolve. Only select those solutions that really will solve the problem you have.

2   Evaluate and eliminate the no-hopers. Don't be too hasty in rejecting unusual ideas, but there will be some ideas that are impractical.

3   Identify criteria to choose the best solution. The criteria should be easy to apply and use. Don't just use financial criteria, as this will miss out many valuable concepts. A selection of possible criteria are:

- Strategic fit – is it consistent with our organisation's strategy?
- Motivation and interest – is it something we want to do?
- Fit with requirements – will it achieve what it needs to achieve?
- Cost – both cost to achieve and cost to maintain once implemented.
- Ease of application – how simple or straightforward will this be to do?
- Level of risk – what is the likelihood of success? What uncertainties are there?
- Disruption to business of solution – will implementing this solution be easy and risk-free, or will it disrupt the business?
- Capability to deliver – technical competencies, business competencies.
- Financial (NPV (net present value), IRR (internal rate of return), payback period).
- Value to customers – will our customers appreciate this solution?

4   Determine the relative weighting of each criterion.

5   Collect necessary information to make decisions, for example:

- What is the strategy?
- What requirements does this solution have to fulfil?
- For NPV calculations – what is an appropriate discount rate?

6   Apply criteria – the criteria do not have to be applied in depth, but simply to show which ideas are better. Often a simple scale such as high–medium–low is sufficient. At this stage it is not the absolute value that matters, but only the relative value compared to the other ideas.

7   Validate – can you check your assessment with someone else?

8   Check if any ideas can be adapted or re-scoped (scoping is described on page 70) to give a different value.

9   Choose the best idea(s).

Converting ideas into actions

Ideas only become valuable when they are converted into actions that can be implemented in reality. Actions have to be defined (*what*), someone has to be named to do them (*who*), there has to be a way to do each action (*how*), and a time frame for completion should be set (*when*).

1 Ensure the idea is understood in sufficient detail to progress (or return to page 45).

2 Minimise divergence. Divergence is valued when creating solutions – now make it converge and try to focus the idea into a limited area. Limit the scope – remove bells and whistles. What are the core elements of the idea you have to implement to achieve your goals?

3 For every aspect of the idea, ask how it will be done and who will do it.

4 If the idea is too big to answer how and who, break it down into smaller activities. Continue to do this until you can answer what, how and who for each activity.

5 Check across all the activities, and:

- Make sure there are no gaps – all necessary parts are done and together they will achieve the idea.
- Make sure there are no overlaps – each activity is done only once.
- Clarify who is responsible overall for making the idea happen.

6 For each action, set a time by which it should be completed.

7 Start work and monitor progress. Amend what, how, who and when depending on the result of each activity.

brilliant recap

Whether you are overcoming a simple problem, seizing a huge opportunity, or implementing a complex solution, the key to success is your clarity of understanding and your ability to clearly define to others what you want in a way they understand.

PART 2

Managing projects

A project is a great way to organise those tasks that are too large, too complex or just too different to be managed as part of your normal work. Project management is very versatile and can be applied to anything from endeavours taking a few days to major activities taking years.

This part considers selecting, scoping, planning, managing, delivering and benefiting from projects. It provides hints, tips and tools to deliver projects easily and successfully.

There are seven chapters in this section:

4 **Project selection** – choosing which projects to undertake and ensuring you are able to deliver them.

5 **Project definition** – defining a project in detail.

6 **Project initiation** – starting projects.

7 **Controlling projects** – managing projects during delivery.

8 **Completing projects and implementing deliverables**
   – finishing projects properly and comprehensively.

9 **Learning from projects** – learning from projects
   once they are complete.

10 **Core project management tools and processes** –
   tools that can be used throughout a project's life.

CHAPTER 4

Project selection

There are always more ideas for projects than there is capacity to do them. So, before starting any project, it's a good idea to confirm it should be done. Project selection is an important part of an organisation's governance. Having selected a project, the checklists on pages 60 and 61 will help in ensuring you have the ability to deliver it.

Developing a project business case

Projects are approved via a business case. A business case provides the information to answer the question *why should a project be invested in*? It explains what the project is, why it should be done, what it will take to do, the benefits and costs of doing it, and any other information needed to decide whether to do the project or not.

Any significant project, or one that requires the use of shared resources such as IT staff, will need a business case. To develop a business case:

1   Find out if there is a standard business-case format to use. Most businesses have standard business-case templates for different types of investments.

2   Choose the template appropriate for the type and scale of investment your project will require. A minor project should only require a 1–2-page business case. A major programme may require significant effort to create the business case, to be contained in a long document with several chapters.

3   Make sure you understand the objectives of the project. If the objectives are not clear, even the most positive business case should not be pursued.

4   Identify benefits:

- Financial benefits – revenue, cost reductions, cost avoidance.
    - Use your organisation's financial approach, e.g. do you calculate NPVs? If so, what discount rate should you apply?
- Other measurable benefits – customer service, staff satisfaction, fault rates, complaint levels, etc.
    - Try to focus on benefits that are related to the business's key performance indicators.
- Intangible benefits – strategic alignment, competency improvement.
    - Not everything is financial, and not everything is measurable – but try to make intangible benefits as realistic and meaningful as possible.

5   Identify costs:

- The costs to run and deliver the project. Staff costs, consumables, external staff, any facilities you must hire for the project, e.g. office space.
- Costs for any investment the project has to make (normally capex or capital costs).
- Operating costs that the organisation will incur once the project is delivered.

6 Write text supporting the project:

- Why is the project being done, what will it achieve, how will it achieve this?
- What is the level of risk in the project – delivery, implementation and business risks?
- What assumptions have been made to create the business case?
    - Check they are reasonable and consistent with others made in the organisation.
- What sensitivities exist in the business case?
    - Some aspects of benefits and costs may vary with limited impact on the business case, others may only alter by a small percentage to change the business case from positive to negative or vice versa.

7 Think what the key questions will be about this project. Try to answer them in the business case. Who reviews and approves business cases? What will they need to know to make a decision one way or another?

8 Identify who will sponsor the business case. This needs to be a manager of sufficient seniority to be a credible sponsor of a project of this scale. For a small project this may be a junior line manager; for the largest programme it must be an executive, perhaps even the CEO.

9 Ask the sponsor, and anyone else who will read it with an open mind, to review the business case and advise you.

- Does it make sense?
- Would he or she approve it?
- Are there any inconsistencies or ambiguities that need to be sorted out?
- What questions does he have on reading it?
- Update and enhance the document accordingly.

10 Check review and business case approval process. Submit the business case.

11 Manage the business approval process:

- Involve yourself and make sure you understand progress through the process.
- Keep your sponsor briefed and make sure she knows what meetings to attend.
- Check that the project is being discussed at the right meetings.
- Be ready to answer questions and overcome objections. Develop presentations to support business case approval as necessary.

Aligning projects with business needs

If an organisation is going to invest in a project, it must be a relevant project that is truly aligned to the needs of the business. Alignment is a judgement requiring debate with project stakeholders.

To see if the project is aligned, and to determine what must be done to align it if it is not, try to answer the following questions:

1   What will this project deliver that is of value to this organisation?

2   Do you understand the organisation's strategy?

   • Is this project aligned consistently with it? (See page 237.)

   • Having finished the project, will the organisation be nearer to achieving its strategy?

3   Does this project solve a problem or fulfil some mandatory requirement such as a legal or regulatory ruling?

   • Why is the problem that this project solves important for this organisation now?

4   Is the way the project solves a problem or takes an opportunity really the best way?

5   Is the opportunity cost of this project worth bearing?

   • What alternative uses could the resources this project will require be put to?

   • Is the project a better investment than any alternative?

Gaining buy-in for a project

Projects need the support of managers and staff in the organisation.

1   Be prepared by being able to answer the three questions:
   - Why is it important to achieve the goal this project will achieve?
   - Why is this project the best way to achieve this goal?
   - Why is this project a better use of the resources than alternative investments?

2   Think through challenges this project may face, and work out how you will overcome them. (See page 217.)
   - Will people generally like or dislike the project? How will you use or overcome this?
   - Will people generally understand the project and what it is trying to achieve? How will you use or overcome this?
   - Are there any rules or assumptions (explicit or unspoken) in this organisation that this project will challenge? How will you reassure people?
   - Is the project in competition for resources with other initiatives? How will you show that this project is a better use of the resources?
   - Is the organisation capable of doing this project? Has anything similar been done successfully or unsuccessfully before? How will you build on or learn from that experience?

3   Identify the stakeholders in the project:
   - Who will benefit from the project?
   - Who will suffer through the project?
   - Who else is interested in the project?
   - Think about internal customers, internal suppliers, users, financiers, staff and who benefits or loses from the project. Should you consider anyone external to the firm – such as customers, trade unions, suppliers?

4   Understand power, influence and attitude towards the project of each of the stakeholders:

- Power and influence: how capable are each of the stakeholders of disrupting or helping this project?

- Attitude: how likely is each of the stakeholders to help or disrupt the project?

5   Categorise the groups of stakeholders:

- High power and influence with positive attitude to the project: try to get them to support the project actively and to work to overcome any resistors.

- High power and influence with negative attitude to the project: try to overcome their objections. If this is not possible, use your supporters to block their influence.

- Low power and influence with positive attitude to the project: try to choose your project team from this group.

- Low power and influence with negative attitude to the project: use general communications and presentations to try and convince.

6   Focus on the most important groups or individuals and determine action to utilise the support and overcome any resistance to the project.

7   Engage in dialogue with prioritised stakeholders:

- Gain commitment for support from important stakeholders.

- Set expectations to a realistic position. Often simply discussing the project and explaining what it will really do is enough to overcome some objections.

- Respond – and, if necessary, amend the project.

8   Build ongoing stakeholder and expectations management into your work for the project. Gaining buy-in for a project is essential at the start of the project and throughout the project's life.

Is this a project or not?

Not all tasks are best delivered as a project. There are no absolute rules on whether something is a project or not, but there are some criteria which can indicate if a project is the best way to complete the task.

It is a project because the task . . .	It is not a project because the task . . .
• is of sufficient complexity that the overhead of a project is justified • can be defined in terms of an objective or outcome required • has a clear beginning and an end • will take a finite amount of time • has a degree of uniqueness and there is no existing process which will adequately end up with the desired result.	• is too small to justify the overhead of project management • is continuous and does not have an end goal or objective, e.g. improving quality on an ongoing basis • has an existing process which will do it • is better done as part of normal operations – such as for continuous performance improvement • does not have even vague scope or objectives (you can run an exploration project to determine objectives).

There are alternatives to projects. The boundary between a project and the alternatives is not absolute. The following table gives a flavour to the alternatives:

Operational task	Ongoing continuous, routine and repetitive tasks, often following a defined process, and managed by adherence to process performance measures.
Business-as-usual change	Small improvements that are done as part of day-to-day work, in which the overhead of a project is not justified. Some improvisation is necessary, but this can be done by staff in line roles.

→

Task forces activities	A group asked to focus on improving an aspect of performance (also called hit squads or performance improvement teams). Task force members may work full- or part-time. At task force meetings, performance is analysed and suggestions for improvements are made. The task force members implement the suggestions and monitor the outcomes as part of their normal job. Task forces work across organisational boundaries, bringing people together to see how activity in one part of an organisation impacts on activity elsewhere.
Facilitated workshops	Workshops can be used to resolve problems and find novel and creative ways of solving issues. (Workshops can be a part of a project.)
Continuous improvement	Ongoing incremental enhancements and tweaking of operational processes in life. Often done under a total quality management (TQM) banner. Each action usually has only a small incremental benefit, but over time continuous improvement will make a significant change.

Critical success factors for projects

There are factors that are fundamental to project success, called *critical success factors* or *CSFs*. At the start of the project, think about CSFs.

Lists of CSFs can go on and on. There are many context-specific success factors. This checklist is based on factors that are important in most situations. If a project is non-compliant with a particular CSF it may still succeed, but the project manager must focus on that area.

A project is most likely to be successful if it has:

- Clear project objectives and explicit success criteria.
- Sufficient senior management support, including a project sponsor with sufficient time to allocate to the project.
- A valid and robust business case, with well-understood sensitivities and risks.
- Involved stakeholders and customers.
- Supportive stakeholders and customers.
- An able project manager, capable of managing this type of project, of this scale, in this type of environment.
- An appropriate project strategy.
- A project plan of sufficient detail.
- The right type and scale of resources including the project team.
- Well-chosen team members who will work constructively as a team.
- Clear roles and responsibilities for the project team members (including between the project manager and project sponsor).
- Ongoing communication by the project manager that keeps everyone informed.
- Ongoing communication by the project team that informs the project manager of what is going on.
- Good progress monitoring.
- Ongoing interaction and feedback to project team members.
- Appropriate use of the right project management processes, e.g. issue management, risk management, change control.
- A project manager who understands CSFs and creates an environment that is consistent with them.

There are checklists throughout the book that will help with each of these.

Project management processes checklist

This checklist contains questions about your project management capability and the situation of the project you are currently running. If you answer No to a question, the relevant checklists can be referenced to help you with this activity.

	Yes	No
Do you have the project scope defined (see pages 65–71)?	☐	☐
Do you know the project requirements (see pages 72–77)?	☐	☐
Do you have a good project plan (see pages 84–88 and 98)?	☐	☐
Do you have the team and resources you need (see pages 81–83 and 97)?	☐	☐
Do you have a way to track and manage progress (see pages 107–112)?	☐	☐
Do you have a format for a progress report (see page 107)?	☐	☐
Do you know how to run progress review meetings (see page 110)?	☐	☐
Do you have a way to manage internal and external dependencies (see page 113)?	☐	☐
Do you have a contingency plan (see page 114)?	☐	☐
Do you need help from your sponsor (see page 115)?	☐	☐
Is your team, including suppliers, motivated and working well (see pages 117, 120 and 122)?	☐	☐
Do you have a way to manage quick wins (see page 119)?	☐	☐
Are you comfortable with how you should implement deliverables and finish the project (see Chapters 8 and 13)?	☐	☐

→

	Yes	No
Are you comfortable that you will optimise what you learn from the project (see Chapter 9)?	☐	☐
Do you have a way to track and manage assumptions (see page 163)?	☐	☐
Do you have a way to track and manage issues (see page 160)?	☐	☐
Do you have a way to track and manage risks (see pages 151–159)?	☐	☐
Do you have a process for change control (see page 165)?	☐	☐
Are you comfortable that you know how to manage stakeholders (see page 166)?	☐	☐
Do you have adequate project administration in place (see pages 168–174 and 207)?	☐	☐
Do you have the right project performance metrics in place (see page 170)?	☐	☐
Do you know all the more advanced project management tools available (see page 172)?	☐	☐
Do you know how to deal with multiple projects and programmes (see Chapter 11)?	☐	☐
Do you have a way to track and manage benefits delivery (see Chapter 14)?	☐	☐

brilliant recap

Effective organisations select the projects best aligned with business needs. As projects are selected they put the right processes and tools in place, and ensure chosen projects meet as many CSFs as possible.

Project definition

Chapter 5 contains checklists to help with defining a project in detail.

Introduction

Project managers create structure and reduce risk by developing clarity and removing uncertainty and ambiguity. They understand the goals, deliverables and scope of the project. This understanding is written into a document known as a *project definition*, *project scope*, *project initiation document*, or some similar title.

Creating a project definition can be tough. Often project customers know they want something, but they are not sure what it is, or cannot explain it in a clear way. Different stakeholders may have incompatible views of the project. Understanding how the project should be defined is made easier by asking well-structured questions.

The definition may be reached quickly and be stable for the life of the project. On the other hand, the whole project may be an exploration in which the definition continuously modifies as the project progresses.

Project definitions have to be sufficiently detailed to allow the project to progress. As the project progresses, the level of detail needed increases. This detailing of definitions as a project progresses is called *progressive elaboration*. If components of the project definition change, this is controlled via *change control* (see Chapter 10).

Determining project objectives

It is essential to have a clear understanding of a project's objective(s), as it sets the direction for the whole endeavour. An objective should answer the question *why* the project is being done, but not *what* or *how* it will be done. A project should have at least one objective, written in the form of short statements, sometimes only one sentence long.

Objectives are best defined with input from stakeholders and the project sponsor.

1   Start by thinking through why the project is being done. What will it achieve? This should not be a broad intention, but a specific, unambiguous and clear goal. Discuss the objective with parties interested in the project.

2   Ask the question – if this objective was met would the organisation be different from how it is today?

3   If there are multiple objectives are they consistent and compatible? A project to increase staff satisfaction is not usually compatible with one to reduce headcount, whereas a project to improve customer satisfaction is compatible with one to improve product quality.

4   Write down the objective. If you cannot write it down it is not yet a useful or usable objective.

5   You should be able to write it in one or two sentences. An objective that takes several lines to write down is usually not one but multiple objectives. If your objective is long, separate it into its component parts.

6   Make sure that the objective is of sufficient quality. Get the wording right. A quality objective is:
   - correct
   - clear
   - meaningful
   - unambiguous
   - concise.

7   Do a common-sense check – is this objective something worthwhile for the organisation to achieve?

8   Review and confirm the objective with the project sponsor and key stakeholders.

9   Produce a final documented version of the objective(s) and put it under change control.

Exploring customer needs

Understanding customer needs can be difficult. Customers do not always know what they want, can't explain it, and disagree among themselves. It is rarely a matter of a quick chat during which customers state all their needs. Needs have to be explored.

An understanding of customer needs supports the development of the project scope. It is not yet necessary to have a detailed definition of every aspect of the project's outcome. In some projects the definition of customer needs will be enough to deliver the project, while in others detailed and specific definitions of what deliverables must achieve are required. These detailed definitions are known as *requirements* (see page 77).

1   Identify the project's important stakeholders (see pages 56 and 166). You cannot talk to everyone who might have a view on a project, but must select those whose views are critical. Agree who the key stakeholders are with the project sponsor.

2   Start to understand needs, by asking the project sponsor and key stakeholders:
   - What are your goals in pursuing this project?
   - What will you be able to do when this project is over that you cannot do now?
   - What shape or form do you expect the deliverables to have?
   - Do you require a specific set of deliverables, or do you require the capability to do something?
   - How do you envisage the deliverables being used or applied in real life?
   - Are these completely unfulfilled needs, or are they needs that are partially fulfilled now?
   - What other expectations do you have?

3   Determine the customer needs with regard to:
   - Maximum project budgets and time frames.
   - Their level of personal involvement in the project.

- Type and scale of resources they may be willing to provide, including project team members.
- Risk they are willing to accept – both in terms of the project itself and of disruption that the project may cause.
- Any other specific needs or constraints upon the project.

4   Identify any conflicts or incompatibilities of customer needs. With the help of the project sponsor, resolve them.

Discovering success criteria

The word *discovering* is used deliberately. Although success criteria may seem obvious, it is only after some time that they are fully understood. Success is a slippery concept and opinions on it vary.

Having success criteria enables you to answer the question – *how will you know when you have achieved your objective?* If you can't answer this question, it is impossible to know if you are doing the right things. Answering this question at the start ensures that the project is designed to meet the success criteria.

It is easy to assume you have achieved an objective because you have done some tasks, but to be really successful you need to have some way of measuring the impact of the actions you have taken. Some examples of success criteria are:

- The project plan uses the planned amount of resources over the planned schedule.
- The project creates the deliverables that fulfil the defined customer needs and requirements.
- The project meets quality standards such as ISO 2000, or it works in the expected way to expected project management process, e.g. a company-defined process or a standard method such as Prince 2. (Prince 2 is a widespread process-based project management methodology, originally developed by the UK's OGC (Office of Government Commerce). It is often mandatory in public sector projects in the UK, and it is fairly common in the private sector too.)
- The project meets its business case.
- The project achieves stakeholder satisfaction. The project delivers what is expected or needed by the stakeholders in a way that they are satisfied with.
- The project is the right project to choose. (This is a measure of success in applying portfolio management rather than a measure of success in applying project management.)

Success criteria can *only* be determined by dialogue with project stakeholders, who may have different opinions. The project sponsor should be the overall owner for the success criteria. Success criteria can be determined by:

1   Identifying the project's important stakeholders. (See pages 56 and 166.)

2   Working with the stakeholders to define and agree how success is to be defined.

3   Ensuring success criteria are documented and explicit.

4   Prioritising across and balancing between success criteria. Which are the most important? Are there any levels of flexibility in some criteria, but not in others? Remove any conflicts or ambiguities.

5   Agreeing when success will be assessed. Success does not happen at one time in a project but is related to events and accumulation of outcomes over time. Will success be measured during the project, when it completes, or afterwards?

6   Agreeing who will do the measurement, if success will be measured after a project is completed.

7   Performing ongoing stakeholder and expectations management through the life of the project. Success factors should be subject to change control.

Defining a project's scope

The *project scope* sets the shape for a project. It defines the boundaries in terms of what is in the project and what is not. It provides a description of the outputs to be provided by the project. It explains what you expect to deliver to your customers when the project is complete. Scope provides a collection of information you need before you can develop an activity and resource plan for your project.

Organisations and methodologies often have template scoping documents. The best way to define scope is by trying to answer a series of questions that make use of the information created through checklists – see pages 65–69.

- What is the overall objective of the project? (See page 65.)
- What are the deliverables? (See page 66.)
  - Are you working to deliver a finite set of deliverables or provide some business capability?
  - Are you working to deliver a set of independent deliverables or an integrated end-to-end solution?
  - How will the quality of deliverables be determined?
  - Are there any deliverables required by the project that it is explicitly not responsible for?
- Are you working to implement a specific solution, or to solve a problem?
  - Are you responsible for the delivery of deliverables or for achieving the business benefits?
- How is the customer going to measure success at the end of the project? (See page 68.)
- What from the customers' viewpoint can be modified?
  - Is predictability more important, or speed to deliver?
- Are there any other constraints on the project?
  - Are there any currently known issues, risks or opportunities?
  - Are there any external considerations?

- How does your customer want to work with you?
    - How will decisions be made on the project?
    - How high is the project in your customer's overall priorities?
    - Can your sponsor allocate all resources the project requires or do other stakeholders need to be involved?
    - Who can legitimately put requirements upon the project?
- Are there any implicit requirements, assumptions or needs that the customer has that are not defined in the scope or requirements documents?

Exploring the iron triangle of time–cost–quality

The *iron triangle* of project management is made up of time, cost and quality. A project takes a certain time and cost to be delivered to a given level of quality (or scope). As there is risk associated with projects, project managers may have to change one or more dimensions of the iron triangle. If something goes wrong the project usually lengthens, costs more, or delivers less. To make the right decisions project managers have to know whether time, cost and quality can be modified.

Developing an understanding of the optimal balance of the iron triangle is best achieved by dialogue with project stakeholders. This understanding underpins planning and management of a project.

1   Determine any absolute boundaries for time, cost or quality, e.g.:

   - Is there a cost at which the project's business case is no longer valid, or a maximum amount of money available?

   - Is there a point in time after, which, if the project is delivered late makes it worthless?

   - What is the minimum level of quality or scope acceptable to customers?

2   Explore, with the project sponsor and key project customers, general preferences for flexibility:

   - If you had no other choice would you prefer to change the cost, the time or the quality of the project?

   - Try to understand the degree of trade-off preferred, e.g. would you rather the cost increased by 5 per cent or time by 10 per cent?

3   Find any limits to the three areas:

   - How much can time, cost or quality shift under the project manager's discretion?

   - How much can time, cost or quality shift under the project sponsor's approval?

- What are the boundaries at which it is essential to receive stakeholder approval to exceed?

4   Factor this information into developing the project plan and making day-to-day decisions on the project, e.g. if there is a problem is it better to invest a little more resource to overcome it, let it delay the project, or avoid it by reducing the project's scope?

5   At periodic intervals on a long project discuss time–cost–quality with the project sponsor to ensure the right balance is being maintained.

Tips for collecting requirements

Whereas a need is a general statement, a requirement is a precise definition of some facet of a deliverable. For some projects there can be hundreds of pages of requirements. In others, requirements may only be a few lines.

In complex situations, requirements collection is not the job of the project manager, but is the role of a *business analyst*. Business analysts have many ways of identifying requirements. This list just provides some high-level tips.

It is important to understand the difference between a requirement and a solution. A requirement defines *what* a customer needs, it does not define how the customer achieves this. For example, a requirement might be 'I need to keep food cool'; a solution to this could be 'I need a fridge'. 'I need a fridge' is not a requirement.

Requirements define project deliverables. They include descriptions of what a deliverable should be able to do, called *functional requirements*, and definitions of how well the deliverable will work, and include quality, performance and operational aspects called *non-functional requirements*.

Collecting requirements is theoretically simple, but in practice can be very difficult:

1   Identify stakeholders.

2   Determine requirements by interrogating stakeholders. Start early: the earlier you get requirements right, the easier it will be to manage and deliver the project.

3   Analyse requirements – explore and understand individual and cumulative requirements.

4   Document and create requirements specification.

5   Remove conflicting or contradictory requirements and those outside the scope of the project.

6   Ensure that requirements are specific. Vague requirements are not usable.

7   Review requirements:

- It is often necessary to reduce the requirements. Requirements are prioritised relative to each other. The more a requirement contributes towards the project's objectives, the higher its priority. Requirements can be broadly prioritised by categorising them as shown on page 77.

- Requirements not relating to achieving the project's objectives should be eliminated.

8   Accept requirements:

- Stakeholders sign off that the requirements are a true representation of their needs.

- Project manager or sponsor signs these off as the requirements the project will deliver, subject to change control.

A tricky issue is deciding when you have collected enough requirements. Stakeholders can come up with additional requirements for a long period of time. At some point, requirements collection must stop so that the project can progress. Deciding that there are sufficient requirements is a matter of judgement. If you are unsure, ask the question – *if you meet this set of requirements will it produce a meaningful deliverable that will meet the original objectives?*

There are various ways to determine requirements, including:

- Interviews and asking structured questions.
- Brainstorming and other facilitated group sessions.
- Showing examples and prototypes – *If it looked like this would it meet your needs? What needs to change?*

Requirements have to be usable to be helpful to the project. Good requirements are:

- understandable and unambiguous
- meaningful

- correct
- well structured
- traceable to their source
- testable
- comprehensive and complete
- such that they meet the objectives of the project.

Filtering and prioritising between requirements

Projects must be practical and achievable. Requirements collection usually produces more requirements than can be fulfilled in a reasonable time and cost. Some requirements must be filtered out.

The steps in slimming down your requirements list are:

1   Link requirements back to original objectives. If a requirement does not help to meet an objective it should not be included.

2   Categorise the requirements:

   ● 'Must be included' – if these requirements are not included the objectives will not be met.

   ● 'Should be included' – if these requirements are not included the full potential of the objectives will not be achieved.

   ● 'Nice to have' – these are helpful requirements, but they do not achieve the original objectives.

   ● 'Should be rejected' – these are requirements which are inconsistent with the original objectives.

3   Slim down requirements against capability to deliver.

   ● Remove the *'should be rejecteds'*.

   ● Remove as many of the *'nice to haves'* as required to reach a sensible scale of project. Focus on removing the requirements that are most complex, expensive or risky to deliver.

   ● If necessary remove some of the *'should be includeds'* as well.

   ● Sometimes to slim down requirements one needs to develop several versions of a plan, depending on which requirements are chosen to be included or not. (See page 86.)

4   If you find you need to reject some of the *'must be included'* requirements, go back and revisit your objectives with your project sponsor before progressing any further.

5   Create a revised requirements specification and maintain it under change control. (See page 165.)

6   Decide what you are going to do with the requirements that have been rejected. They should be stored for future review as unfulfilled needs. If you have a corporate requirements catalogue then they can be stored there.

Turning requirements into designs

In the project, requirements have to be turned into a *design*. A requirement is an understanding of a need and a design is the definition of the solution to this need. The process and terminology of design are context-specific. A building project would design a solution in a different way from an IT systems development.

At the simplest level, the steps to convert requirements into a design are:

1   Convert stakeholder requirements into a technical definition. The requirements are usually specified in non-specialist language. For someone like an IT developer to convert the requirements into software, they need to be written in relevant technical language.

2   Based on the technical definition, design a solution. This is a combination of a creative exercise and looking at existing solutions to see if they fulfil or can easily be tailored to fulfil the requirements. (This has a big impact on the project plan as it is a major part of the project.)

3   Review the design with the project customers to ensure that it meets their needs. This is an optional step, as in some situations the stakeholders may not have the skills to review a design.

4   Agree how the solution will be tested against the requirements when it is developed (see Chapter 8).

Designs can be developed with or without stakeholder input. Development approaches such as *Agile* encourage working cooperatively with stakeholders. Solutions designers are involved in requirements capture, they help stakeholders to explore requirements and remove any impossible or impractical requirements. Stakeholders are involved in design, which ensures it meets their needs.

brilliant   recap

The foundation stone of every successful project is a clear scope, and a comprehensive set of customer requirements.

CHAPTER 6

Project initiation

Project initiation requires putting the team and other resources in place to deliver the project, developing a project plan, and starting to deliver the project.

The project sponsor

The project sponsor is a key role in every project. The sponsor represents the interests of the project investors and supports the project manager to fulfil his day-to-day role. The project manager manages the day-to-day work on the project.

The project sponsor's role is to:

- Identify the business need for a project, and act as an evangelist for the project.
- Provide senior support to a project during execution:
  - accessing resources
  - overcoming problems
  - decision making – e.g. approving baseline plans, budgets and changes
  - communicating about the project
  - retaining enthusiasm and support for the project within the business. Project managers are dependent on the sponsor's power, authority and influencing skills.
- Set the business context for a project, the project manager and the project team, answering questions like: why is the project important, and how does it fit into the organisation's strategy?
- Ensure that the project manager is managing the project in a competent fashion.
- Take accountability for delivery of business benefits, which may accrue after the project is completed and the project manager has finished her work.

A project sponsor must be of sufficient seniority to support a project of the scale required, and must have enough time available to sponsor the project. Sponsorship is rarely a full-time role. It may only require a few hours a week, but it is a real task and needs active involvement. A project sponsor should:

- Have familiarity with project management concepts and terminology.
- Recognise the relationship between sponsor behaviour and project success.
- Have the ability to probe and question successfully, often forming a picture by taking information from multiple sources.
- Be willing to spend sufficient time understanding the project status.

The project manager

The second key role in a project is the project manager. The project manager has responsibility for delivering all the components of a project. This may or may not be a full-time job, and the work required varies from project to project. Normally, the project manager is responsible for:

- Scoping out the work to ensure there is a clear understanding of why a project is being done, and what it will produce.

- Planning the project and determining what resources are required, how long it will take and how much it will cost.

- Getting the necessary resources allocated and ensuring every project team member knows what they are responsible for.

- Controlling the project and ensuring that it achieves its objectives within the planned time and cost.

- Completing the project properly to make sure everything produced by the project is of the quality expected and works as required.

- Ensuring problems or issues that may cause the completion of tasks to be delayed or stopped are resolved.

Project management is largely a generic approach, but that does not mean all project managers can manage all projects. To manage a specific project, a project manager needs to make use of:

- Project management knowledge and experience, suitable to a project of this type and scale. This includes a capability to:
  - pull objectives and scope together in a situation of ambiguity
  - develop a project business case
  - plan and resource the project
  - monitor and report on project progress
  - drive project progress
  - manage issues, risks, assumptions and changes through the project

- complete the project and hand over deliverables to in-life owners (the operational managers who have to live and work with your project's deliverables once the project is complete).
- ensure the groundwork for the delivery of benefits.

● Context-specific knowledge, both of project and type of organisation. This includes:

- an ability to use the language, terminology and concepts relevant to the situation.
- an understanding of culture, implicit rules, expectations and assumptions of a business.
- skills and knowledge specific to an industry or area of application.

● Personal capabilities, including:

- a feeling of ownership for and involvement in the project.
- a dynamic and positive style of working.
- being results-orientated and having a completer–finisher mentality.
- the ability to handle stress.
- the ability to achieve clarity when there is uncertainty and ambiguity.
- being comfortable with multi-tasking.
- the ability to make reliable judgements.
- sufficient creativity to overcome issues and problems.
- empathy with the project's customer and stakeholders.
- good networking skills.
- political sensitivity and sensitivity to the environment.
- adapting style to the situation.
- a sense of humour is also a great asset!

● General management and leadership skills appropriate to the size and seniority of the project management team. Managing a project team has challenges that are specific to projects, but many of the skills are those generic to any management role, such as team motivation. The leadership role depends on what role the sponsor takes. An active sponsor may fulfil the leadership role in a project, but one who spends little time on the project will not.

Choosing a project strategy and life cycle

Each project is unique and there will be several ways to deliver it. Some approaches will be better than others. It is important to choose an effective and efficient approach to the project.

The *project strategy* defines the overall approach that will be used to reach the project's goals. The *project life cycle* is the series of steps the project will go through to achieve those goals. To determine the project strategy and life cycle:

1   Don't jump to conclusions too quickly. You must choose a strategy and life cycle, but don't just use what you already know. It needs to vary to suit the project. Try to determine whether this strategy and life cycle contribute to the success or failure of the project.

2   If you are unclear about project strategy and project life cycle options, do some research. Talk to experienced project managers. How would they face the challenge of a similar project?

3   Determine the project strategy. How, in broad terms, will you approach meeting the project's objectives and achieving the associated success criteria?

4   Answer the following questions, and any other related questions you can think of:

- Do you understand the problem your project is trying to overcome? If not, the project must include a phase for problem definition.

- Do you understand the solution your project will implement? If not, the project requires phases associated with exploring and selecting the most appropriate solution.

- Will there be a need to design a solution, or will it be about choosing an off-the-shelf option? If the former is preferable, you need a solutions design phase; if the latter is more suitable you may need a tendering and supplier selection stage.

- Will you do the work yourself or will you use a third party? If using a third party you may need a tendering, supplier selection and contracting phase. Also, you must understand the split in management responsibilities between yourself and your supplier(s).
- Do you think it is best to complete the work in one set of sequential steps, or will there be a need to iterate between steps several times? This is related to how much change you expect as the project progresses, and the level of certainty possible at the start of the project.
- What is the most important constraint – time, cost or quality?

5   Choose an appropriate life cycle. What life cycle is most suited to achieving this?

- What is the nature of the project and the environment it runs in, e.g. is it an IT project in a bank, a business change project in an oil company, or a construction project in a water company?
- What is the scale, complexity, degree of novelty and risk associated with the project?
- Is there a standard project life cycle in this business that has to be used?
- What life cycles and approaches have been used in the past?
- Were these effective, and can they be improved?
- Do you want to focus your plan on the steps you will take or the deliverables you will create?

6   Review the strategy and life cycle with the project sponsor and, if possible, an experienced project manager who can provide expert support.

Creating plans using work breakdown structures

A project plan is essential. It:

- Provides an understanding of the activities involved in a project.
- Enables you to understand how long a project will take, what resources will be required and how much it will cost to do.
- Facilitates communicating and explaining the project to project stakeholders and project team members.
- Allows you to allocate work to different people in the project.
- Is the basis for managing your project to successful completion.
- Supports wider business planning and management commitment-making.

There are several ways to create a project plan. A project manager can use one or more of:

- Top-down identification of main chunks, followed by decomposition into constituent parts.
- Group effort/workshops to brainstorm the possible activities, followed by arranging the activities into appropriate chunks and a logical sequence.
- Adaptation of previous plans from similar projects.
- Asking an expert in the area of the project for advice.

Developing a project plan usually starts with the creation of a *work breakdown structure* or WBS. The WBS is a structured hierarchy that provides a way the tasks in a project plan can be organised. The WBS helps in managing the project, communicating about the project, and identifying gaps and overlaps in the project. There are many WBS options, and the choice of WBS is important.

The way to develop a work breakdown structure is to:

1 Determine the basis for the work breakdown structure. What is the most sensible way to group the activities in the project? There are different ways, based on the deliverables from the project, the activities in the project, or the process or life cycle that the project uses.

2 Divide the overall project into its component tasks. One way to do this is to brainstorm a task list, and then arrange the tasks into the WBS. This will probably take several attempts.

3 Continue to divide the component tasks into smaller tasks until you have a comprehensive list of things that must be done to complete the project. The point at which you have gone far enough is when:

   - It is enough for you to be able to manage the work.
   - The detail is sufficient for you to estimate and schedule the project.
   - The tasks are small enough to be allocated to individuals in the team or individual sub-teams within the project team.

4 Review and check the WBS is complete and comprehensive. There should be no gaps or overlaps. Tasks should appear only once in the WBS.

The steps in developing a plan using a WBS are:

5 Select a basis for decomposing a plan (deliverables, along a process, etc.).

6 Define the activities in the WBS.

7 Identify linkages between activities.

8 Estimate duration and resources required for each activity (see page 89), by:

   - asking someone who does know or has previous experience of something similar
   - using any available rules of thumb
   - modelling it against other similar tasks
   - breaking down the task further until you get tasks you can estimate
   - making an assumption but keeping track of it.

9 Review the resources available and the schedule of availability. (See pages 89–97.)

10 Schedule the activities, taking into consideration the linkages, duration and resource availability. This can be done automatically with planning software such as MS Project or Primavera.

11 Add appropriate milestones.

12 Review the plan against objectives and constraints and ensure it is consistent with them. If it is not, revisit the plan and adapt it until it conforms to objectives and constraints. This includes consideration of time, cost and quality constraints and critical success factors.

The alternative is *backwards planning*. Normal planning is called *forward planning* – starting from today, you plan the tasks the project requires and work out the end date. With backwards planning you start with the end date and work backwards, making whatever compromises are required to ensure that the plan can be completed by the chosen end date.

Estimating project times and costs

A plan shows how long the project will take and how much it will cost. This information is useful for budgeting for projects, for managing projects in life, and to support making business commitments. Estimation is often the hardest part of developing a project plan.

There are several ways to develop estimates (time and costs) for projects:

- Top-down and comparative estimates: a summary estimate for the whole project. This is normally based on the assessment of an experienced practitioner who can make comparisons to similar projects.
- Bottom-up: using the WBS and estimating the resources required for each activity in the WBS, and then totalling across the project.
- Expert input: support and advice from an expert in one or more areas of the project.
- Parametric: using a sizing algorithm or heuristic for a type of work. Such algorithms exist for IT, construction and many engineering projects.
- Risk-based: there are different ways of including a consideration of risk in project estimates, e.g. PERT.

The most common way is a bottom-up estimate, which is then compared to a common-sense judgement from a top-down basis. To perform a bottom-up estimate:

- Complete the work breakdown structure (see page 86).
- For each task in the WBS, estimate its duration and resources required. (See page 90 for more information on costs.)
- If you cannot estimate, you must:
  - break the task down into further levels of detail until you can estimate; or
  - ask someone who does know; or
  - make an assumption. This is usually necessary for parts of the plan, but each assumption increases the risk of the project.

- Having made all the estimates, add in contingency to take account for the level of risk. The risk is associated with how much is uncertain about the project. The more unknowns or novelty, the greater the percentage of contingency required. Contingency should be included within your estimates for time and cost. Uncertainty is not just about the risk of error for each task in the WBS, but also the risk that the WBS has omissions. The smaller the amount of contingency there is, the more likely the project is to overrun and the more precise management control is required.

It is important to be able to cost a project so that appropriate authorisation can be gained, a budget can be provided, and expectations set as to how much the project will cost. (See also page 235.) There are four types of costs associated with a project:

1   Costs associated with doing the work on the project, which can be derived from the project plans, e.g.:
    - Human resource costs – people's time working on the project. This is both internal resources (if time is tracked and costed back to a budget), and external resource charges. You need to consider how people's time is charged (by hour/day/week), the cost per unit, and how many units will be used.
    - Things you have to buy or rent to do the project. For example, you may rent a room for the project team to work in, and may buy some project management software to help run the project.
    - Consumables used on the project, e.g. stationery.

2   Costs associated with things you must buy to create the deliverables. These costs can be determined from the design documents and include:
    - capital investments; and
    - materials used in the production of deliverables.

3   Costs associated with running the deliverables after the project is complete (e.g. maintenance costs) or dealing with the impact of the project (e.g. redundancy or recruitment costs). Normally, these are not costs a project has to budget for, but are paid for out of departmental or operational budgets. However, a project may be expected to pay for the operation of deliverables for some period after completion, e.g. the first year after implementation.

4   Overhead costs in a business that will be reallocated. Some businesses reallocate some overhead costs to projects, e.g. for facilities. A project manager must be aware of this to take account of it in the project budget. Talk to your finance department.

The project manager must develop a budget which shows the amount of money required and the rate of spend. The budget must take account of the various accounting treatments of different categories of spend.

Identifying the skills, roles and organisation required

The work on a project is done by the project team. Building a project team starts by developing an understanding of the skills and roles required.

1   Review the work breakdown structure. What types of tasks are there, and therefore what skills and capabilities are needed?

2   Review the overall project plan. What volume of these skills is needed?

- How many people with each skill set do you need? How long will you need them for?

- Are you likely to find anyone who is cross-skilled and could fulfil multiple roles on the project?

3   Once you have some idea of the people you need to complete the project, you will need to define how they will be organised for the project. There is no right or wrong answer, but the factors you need to consider are:

- Size of project – the larger the project, the more you will need a formal structured organisation with clear roles and management levels.

- Stage of a project – the organisation may adapt as the project progresses. A project in a feasibility stage, during implementation, or during post-implementation support may have different needs.

- Complexity of the work – is everyone doing very similar tasks or is there a large variation?

- Type of staffing – are they dedicated or part-time? Are they junior technicians or senior specialists like lawyers? Each need to be managed in different ways.

- Third-party involvement – are you outsourcing some or all of the project work?

- Relationship to end-users – are you working with end-users during the project, or are you separate from them and will hand over once the project is complete?

Common examples of project organisational structures you may use are:

- Based on the functions in the project team – e.g. engineering, marketing, legal and project management.
- Based on the deliverables to be created – e.g. IT system, business process, organisational units.
- Based on stakeholder organisation – e.g. reflecting the structure of the organisation the project is being run in.
- Based on geography – e.g. North team and South team.
- Based around the phases if it is a multi-stage project – e.g. phase 1 team, phase 2 team, etc.
- Based around the structure of the project plan. This is usually the best way to organise a project team, as it makes allocating work to teams easiest, and ongoing project management more straightforward.

4   For larger projects with many people working on them organised into separate sub-teams of the overall project team (see also Chapter 11):

- Determine if the sub-teams need team leaders to interface to the project manager. Usually they will.
- Determine if each sub-team needs its own project managers.
- Agree how the individual sub-teams will be allocated work and will report progress to the overall project manager.

Choosing the project team

There is a big difference between knowing what sort of people you want and choosing your project team – knowing you need an engineer with a certain skill-set is different from having person x, who has the ideal skills and attitudes, allocated to the team.

1   Start by applying the following principles to team selection:

  - Be willing to adapt your project team structure to the reality of the human resources available.

  - Fewer of the right people are much better than more of the wrong. Quality wins out over quantity when it comes to team selection.

  - Don't think that the resolution to every problem is to add more resource. Adding resource reduces the workload on others on the project and may make tasks possible that otherwise are not – but each additional resource increases management complexity. There comes a point at which adding more resource reduces, rather than increases, efficiency and effectiveness.

  - It is better to have fewer more highly motivated people than more unmotivated people.

  - Try to get resourcing levels right at the start. You may be able to add resources later, but this may cause more disruption than benefit.

2   Work closely with resource owners (generally line managers) to get the necessary people allocated to the project. Be prepared to negotiate.

3   Where line managers cannot provide the resources you need, look to external sources – but you have to have the budget to cover the associated costs.

4   Review your staffing options. If you have no choice, then you will have to work with the people offered. If you have choices, start to select the best people you can. 'Best' in this context is a balance of factors:

  - Are they available for the duration of the project?

  - Are they available 100 per cent of their time or not? If not, will they have to multi-task on this project and other activities they have to do? If so, is this reasonable and manageable? Talk to the individuals, not just their managers. You want to understand real availability, not theoretical.

- Are they the right people to do the individual tasks that will be allocated to them, considering skills, competency, attitude and motivation?
- Do they have effective styles of interaction and communication?
- Will they work productively as part of a team? Consider cultural fit, effect on other team members and team skills.
- Can you afford them?

5   Update your theoretical project team structure (from page 92) to what you really have.

6   Aggregate resource usage across the plan to understand your points of overload and underload. Focus on the resources that are continuously overloaded as this is the key risk area. The information on over- and underloaded resource is used to re-plan and reschedule.

7   Reiterate the plan, taking account of the actual resources available, which may be different from your original request. You may reiterate between planning and resourcing several times.

Some tips on managing the team:

- A team is not simply a collection of individuals, but is a dynamic unit of competencies, attitudes and relationships. A bad team is less productive than the individuals will be separately. A good team will be several times as productive.

- Building a team and making it fully productive takes time and willingness for the team members to interact productively.

- Sometimes there will be disagreement or conflict. This is not always bad. Conflict can generate brilliant thinking, clear the air and resolve issues. But it needs to be controlled, as it can become destructive.

- Watch out for groupthink, where the team becomes so aligned that everyone sees everything the same way. A strong team has diversity of views and encourages open debate between team members.

- A team needs to be led. This is part of the central role of the project manager. A project manager who cannot lead the project team will not be effective. This requires power and influence over the team members. The project manager should:

- assign work
- monitor progress and performance
- watch behaviour and take appropriate action
- identify and resolve team problems
- consult team members for advice – but make her own decisions
- give and receive feedback
- modify leadership style to that needed for different team members.

Other project resources

Projects may consume a variety of other resources which have to be factored into plans and budgets. The project manager should:

1 Determine what other project resources you need, considering:

- equipment
- facilities
- consumables
- services.

2 Determine if you have to pay for any of these other resources.

3 Determine if you have the budget to cover the costs. If not, look for alternatives, or discuss with your sponsor if there is a way to increase the budget.

4 Identify where you get the resources from/order them through/who you can book them through.

5 Determine the lead times for delivery/availability/booking and ensure these times are factored into the project plan.

6 For any critical equipment, facilities or consumables for which you are uncertain, determine what you will do if it does not arrive or become available.

Creating a communications plan

Communication is central to the project manager's role. Communication should be planned and executed in a structured way. Informal dialogue should be encouraged, but it should be consistent with the messages that need to be communicated.

Communication is important because:

● it is the basis of managing people's expectations.

● it helps the project team to determine if they are doing the right things.

● it facilitates the occurrence of necessary changes.

● it enables the project manager to collect feedback on the project. This is essential for progress monitoring as well as issue and risk management.

● it can keep support for the project going, and is essential for good change management.

The approach to communications has to be structured according to the scale and sensitivity of the project. For a large programme of work, it is essential to develop a communications plan that runs alongside the main project plan. The steps to do this are:

1 Allocate responsibility for communications. Normally, this is part of the project manager's role, but in complex situations it may be allocated to one of the project team members or to a dedicated communication manager.

2 Develop key messages. What are the main overall messages about the project?

3 Identify target stakeholders. Who needs to be communicated to about this project?

4 Identify the key events on the project plan. These are events that stakeholders need to be aware of or prepared for. What needs to be explained and when?

5 Build a communications activity list. This is formed by cross-referencing key events to the target stakeholders. For each event/stakeholder combination, determine what actions need to be undertaken to communicate, and when.

6 Determine media. What is the best format for these communication activities?

It may be that one-to-one conversations are required: a presentation, team meetings, mass emails, company magazine articles, etc. Generally, the more tailored to the individual the more effective the communication, but the more work it is to do.

7 Determine timings. When should the messages be delivered for most impact? How many times should they be repeated?

8 Allocate responsibility. Who will create which communications materials, and who will present them?

9 Start working to the communication plan.

10 Review and amend the communication plan as the project progresses. The plan needs to be dynamic. Not all communications will be effective and some will result in unexpected outcomes. You must be prepared to handle this.

Don't underestimate the importance of communication. It is central to many projects and essential for achieving sustained change. But don't overestimate communications. It is not the same as delivering the project. Communications will not save a flawed project, but flawed communications can doom a project.

Mobilising a project team and running a kick-off meeting

Mobilisation is the responsibility of the project manager. The objectives of mobilisation are:

● To energise and align the project team. If it is a large project team this may take some considerable effort.

● To ensure the broader stakeholder community is supportive of the project and ready for it.

● To ensure project team members understand the objectives of their involvement, the work that has been allocated to them, and how they fit within the overall plan.

Once this is done, project delivery can commence. To mobilise the project team you should:

1 Brief line managers providing resource to the project as to when resource will be required. Set expectations that project plans are not exact and these timescales may change.

2 Ensure that every member of the project team knows:

   ● Their role in the project and what tasks they are responsible for doing.

   ● How their task fits into the overall project.

   ● What to do when they have completed initial work (i.e. what they should do next).

   ● Their responsibilities with regard to project management processes – especially those associated with progress reporting, issue and risk management and change control.

   ● The level of input expected. This includes clarifying whether they are part-time or full-time, and what happens to their normal workload.

3 Deal with any of the project team's concerns.

4 Ensure that the project team is motivated, ready to start work, and has the supporting materials, equipment or facilities they need.

5 Brief the project sponsor so he is aligned with the project and ready to provide the support and direction required.

6 Ensure that key customers and stakeholders are prepared for the start of the project and ready to provide any support required to the project. The key customers must know when this support will be needed.

7 Brief anyone else whose actions or support are important to the project's success.

8 Check that the project is approved, budget allocated and prioritised as part of the organisation's portfolio of projects.

9 Set up any project infrastructure required, such as an online document library, time reporting systems, templates and documents.

10 Run a project kick-off session with the whole project team to set expectations and make sure everyone is starting out in the right direction.

The kick-off session is the responsibility of the project manager. A typical agenda for a kick-off session, which should be tailored to your situation, is:

1 Introduction to the project by the project sponsor, explaining the business context and importance of the project.

2 Team-building exercise 1 – for project team members to start to get to know each other. Something energising and quick.

3 Presentation by project customers on how the project will improve their work.

4 Team-building exercise 2 – something fun to break up the monotony of presentations.

5 Project manager presents the plan and initiates discussion on whether this is the right plan for this project.

6 Project manager describes the objectives, scope and success criteria for the project.

7 Break the group into teams of 4–8 people for workshop sessions. The workshops are used to explore:

- Project plan – each group may review specific segments of the overall plan.
- Risks that can be identified.

- Issues the group identify.
- Any ways the project can be improved.

8 Brief feedback from workshop sessions to the whole group.

9 Presentation by the project manager or project office manager to introduce expected working processes, document templates, etc. This should be a short session. It is not a training course, but should overview what is required and how to find more information.

10 Question and answer session. Questions to be answered by the project manager, project sponsor and key customer representatives.

11 Finish with a motivation talk, covering the key points noted below.

Such a session should be designed to be interactive and fun.

There are a number of key messages to get across in the kick-off session. Many of these will be specific to the project, and should be based on the communications plan. The following points should be reinforced during the kick-off in all projects:

- The project is important.
- The project will only be successful with the project team's hard work.
- The working and team style required to make the project work.
- Expectations as to the likely response to the project team's work.
  - Will the rest of the organisation generally be in favour of or against this project?
  - How should the project team members respond to any unsupportive challenge?
- The project plan provides the framework everyone works to and is measured against.
- Each project team member is responsible for the tasks allocated to them.
- The plan will change in some ways as the project progresses, and at times it may feel more chaotic than the project team members expect. Each project is unique, so there will be some unexpected occurrences.
- Projects rely on information and regular updates on progress, issues, risks, changes and so on. It is everyone's responsibility to keep the project manager informed. This is not an administrative overhead, but an important part of good management.

brilliant recap

Key responsibilities of the project manager are gaining the necessary resources and developing a sufficiently detailed project plan – based on the agreed scope and project definition.

CHAPTER 7

Controlling projects

These checklists will help you to keep your project progressing and support you in reaching your end goals. This represents the core day-to-day work of a project manager.

Tracking progress and writing a progress report

To be able to keep a project on track, the project manager has to monitor progress. There are three questions a project manager must be able to answer to be sure the project is progressing as expected:

- *For schedule*: Is the project progressing at least as fast as planned?
- *For cost*: Is the project's budget being spent no faster than planned? (See page 168.)
- *For benefits*: Are the benefits from the project being delivered at the rate expected?

The last question is only relevant if the project delivers benefit as it progresses and not just at the end.

To track progress against any of these three dimensions you need two sets of information:

- How much work has been completed, how much money has been spent and what benefits have been achieved?
- How much *should* have been completed, spent or achieved?

Being able to answer these questions requires a plan and a budget, and an accurate understanding of progress. If you don't have these, you cannot make an objective assessment of progress – you can only make a subjective judgement which may well be wrong.

Tracking progress is based on the regular collection of information from the project team. A weekly collection is sufficient for most projects. The information should be collected formally through progress reports and informally from chats with project team members.

This information needs to be analysed at two levels:

- relative to the current point in time
- as a trend over time.

You should always expect deviations from the plan. Day-to-day variances in progress are less important than the trend. If the trend in progress is significantly different from the plan, the plan and your approach to the project should be reviewed.

It can also be helpful to track trends over time (also see page 170) in:

- volumes of issues and rate of resolutions
- risk levels
- rate of use of contingency.

A central way to communicate in a project is via progress reports. Good progress reporting helps in managing expectations. Poor progress reports will annoy stakeholders and indicate a badly run project.

1 Identify audiences for progress reports. There may be several audiences, e.g. project team reporting to project manager, project manager reporting to sponsor and key stakeholders, project sponsor reporting to an organisation's board.

2 Check if there are any corporate standards for project reports. If there are, use them.

3 Determine information needs. What do these different audiences need to know, and what would they like to know?

4 Identify sources of information, normally project team members. Work out how often it is practical to collect the information.

5 Define the format of reports: there may be several for different audiences. Make sure reports are specific enough to different audiences, e.g. if you have to produce a progress report for a director she probably wants different information in the report than a project team leader would. But keep the reports as similar as possible to minimise overhead.

6 Develop processes to regularly collect the information. The information must be collected before the report is required and with sufficient time to turn it into a report. If there is a hierarchy of reports then the information needs to be available a few days before the top-level report is produced.

7 Start collecting information and creating reports.

8 Seek feedback and ensure the format is optimal – consider adapting to stakeholder needs, but try to avoid producing tailored versions of reports for individual managers.

9 Ensure a culture develops where reports are produced on a timely basis and to a high standard.

10 Periodically verify the data used to create reports. Unless you do this, there is a risk that you will be fed, deliberately or unintentionally, misleading information.

Usually, projects produce summary weekly reports, and more detailed reports on a less regular basis. A typical set of information in a report is:

- project name
- date and reporting period covered
- summary of progress and status
- main actions completed in last period
- main actions to be completed in next reporting period
- issues for escalation
- risks for escalation
- decisions and approvals required.

Running a project status review session

Project reports provide useful information, but for an accurate understanding of progress a review session is required, where direct dialogue occurs between the project manager and project team members. Reviews are an important part of managing a project.

Before holding a project review, you should determine:

- Why are you having a project review session? What information will you know and what questions will you be able to answer once this review session is complete? What outcomes or types of actions will happen following the meeting? If you cannot answer these questions – do not hold the review.

- Are you reviewing a sensible amount of information, and information that needs debate and discussion?
  - Having a list of 100 questions you want to answer is not a practical meeting that can be completed in a sensible amount of time. Break it into several meetings.
  - If they are simple yes/no questions or factual pieces of information, is it really necessary to have a meeting?

- Who is the review session for? There are differences between an internal review with a project manager and project team, one with the project sponsor, and one with project stakeholders, customers or executives.

The typical aim of a review session is to:

- Verify project reports and get a complete understanding of project status. This includes factual information such as work completed, but also intangible data such as the mood of the project team.

- Determine if remedial actions need to take place to maintain status.

- Identify opportunities to improve the project.

- Discuss plans moving forward and generally share information.

- Reduce the overhead on the project team in terms of reporting. Reporting is a key part of working on a project, but it is not the goal of projects to report. Whoever is running a review session has to balance between too-frequent reviews, creating too great an overhead, and too few, which means that insufficient information is gathered to provide control.

Typical contents of a review session are:

- Informing team of any changes in direction, baseline plans or other relevant information.
- Determining what the team did in the last period. Was it as planned; what was produced?
- Determining what the team plan to do in the next period. Does that match the project plan?
- Discussing upcoming milestones.
- Reviewing plans and making any amendments.
- Checking if there are any new issues, risks or changes the team want to raise.
- Assessing the progress on any issues, risks or changes the team are working on.
- Discussing any team or staff issues that may impact the project.
- Reporting back on actions held by the project manager or escalated for higher support.
- Any other points project team members want to discuss.

For more complex projects and programmes it is worth also reviewing dependencies between projects (see page 113) and any resource issues and conflicts (see page 191).

Following the review meeting you can make decisions about the project. Typical questions you should be able to answer are:

- Are you on track or not? What is the overall project status?
- If not, what will you do to bring the project back on track?
- What is your current view of the likely outcome of the project?
- Is there anything you need to escalate or warn the sponsor about?
- Are there any actions relating to team motivation or management?

Typical actions that may be required following a review session are one or more of the following:

Project team	Project manager	Project sponsor
• Carry on as you are • Try to do subsequent tasks more quickly or more cheaply • Find alternative ways to do what you are doing • Specific actions – e.g. issue or risk management actions • Change focus of activity	• Carry on as you are • Focus management on a specific area • Release some contingency • Change resources in some way • Look at alternative ways to do what you are trying to do • Alter the project in some way • Raise a change request • Escalate to sponsor for help • Re-baseline plan	• Respond to escalation • Provide decision or give direction • Provide approval

Managing dependencies

Dependencies between tasks are important parts of a project plan. Dependencies result in tasks in a plan being done in a certain order. There are two types of dependency:

- Internal dependencies – relationships between tasks within the project plan.

- External dependencies – relationships between tasks within the project and tasks external to a project. The latter may or may not be on another project. These are sometimes called *interfaces*.

It is important for the project manager to monitor and manage dependencies, or else projects can fail. Dependencies should be managed by the following steps:

1. Identify dependencies. It is critical to identify all dependencies.
   - What has to happen for a task to be completed?

2. If dependencies are real they must be in the plan. Try to remove or break the dependency if possible, as dependencies constrain and increase timescales. If they can be removed they should be.

3. Build the plan using the right type of dependency: start to finish, start to start, finish to finish, delay, etc. Wrong dependencies can elongate the plan unnecessarily.

4. For external dependencies ensure you know:
   - What project or piece of work is delivering the dependency? (Try to avoid making assumptions about delivery of dependencies; plan using verified facts.)
   - Who is accountable for delivering the work you are dependent upon?
   - Should the dependency be brought into the scope of the project?

5. Monitor delivery of the dependency by getting periodic updates on progress, so that you can assess the degree of risk upon the project if it is not delivered on time.

6. On critical dependencies, do not accept statements of progress; probe the progress reports as you would any part of your own project to be confident that they are accurate.

7. Update plans in line with progress on delivery of dependencies.

Contingency plans

When a risk cannot be controlled, the alternative is to mitigate the impact it would have should it occur, with a contingency plan. A contingency plan is a series of actions that are only initiated should a risk event occur or when a defined trigger happens.

1   Identify the risk events that you need a contingency plan for (see Chapter 10 for risk management advice).

2   Define the contingency plan. Consult the team and use creativity. The creation of good contingency plans can be hard and needs real creativity.

3   Determine what triggers your contingency plan. It is often assumed that the trigger for a contingency plan to be activated is the occurrence of a risk event. Unfortunately, because of the length of time it takes to implement, many contingency plans have to be activated before the risk occurs. Unless you understand when to implement the contingency plan, it is worthless.

4   Ensure you have the resources to implement the contingency plan, or have a way of getting them should the contingency plan be implemented. Contingency plans are optional expenditure to reduce risk, and may be difficult to justify. Consider them as an investment in insurance.

5   Ensure the contingency plan reduces risk. Some contingency plans sound great, but when analysed can be shown to result in no risk reduction, and so are not worthwhile.

6   Ensure the sponsor and stakeholders understand the implications if the contingency plan is implemented. It may mean more cost, and often means a reduced scope.

7   Monitor for the trigger event, and action the plan should the trigger occur.

8   Maintain or update the contingency plan should the project change in a way that requires it to be updated.

When and how to escalate for help

Project managers cannot solve every problem they encounter. They often need to escalate for help. There is a balance with escalation: escalate as soon as you need to, but only when you need to. If you escalate every time you have problems you are not adding value as the project manager. But if you do not escalate when you should, you are not taking advantage of a valuable resource and may be increasing the risk.

1 Understand the difference between escalation and keeping the sponsor informed.

2 Warn people in advance that you may come to them for help. Most people are open to this if asked nicely. *'Would it be OK if I come to you for help as the project progresses? I won't do it too often, but if I'm stuck would it be OK to get your advice or support?'*

3 Decide, as issues arise, if you need to escalate. You should escalate if:

   - you cannot resolve the issue yourself or with resources under your control/influence

   - it will be significantly easier, quicker or cheaper to escalate than do it yourself

   - it will help with project politics or expectations management if you escalate.

4 Decide who you will escalate to: is it the sponsor, or another line manager? Most escalations will be to the sponsor. But the sponsor is not the only choice; there are many other members of staff who may be able to help you. Make use of your network to solve specific problems.

5 Try to avoid making the request a surprise. If you are going to have to escalate try to link to points made in progress updates. *'As I noted in last week's report . . . so now I need help to . . .'*

6 Work out how you will phrase your request, and what your desired outcome is.

7 Be clear about what you actually need. There are few things more irritating than a vague request for help. Follow the pattern: *'We have an issue . . . The implications are . . . If you could . . . it would be resolved'.*

8 If possible, give options, and try to make the person you are asking feel as if they have a choice. When you hold a gun to someone's head they will do what you ask, but they won't like you for doing it!

9 Choose the best time to ask for help. You can't always choose the timing, but asking for help last thing on a Friday afternoon is less likely to get a positive response than asking at lunchtime on Monday.

10 Request the specific help you need.

11 Monitor results. If the help was effective, thank the sponsor. If not, you may have to do it again or escalate to an even more senior level.

Driving performance in a project team

No matter how brilliant a project manager is, unless the project team members do the work allocated to them the project will fail. A project manager has to be able to drive performance in the project team. A well-managed and motivated team will perform far better than a better resourced and skilled team that lacks motivation.

- Try to pick people who are motivated or interested in the project in the first place.
- Assign clear roles and responsibilities related to individuals' capabilities and wants. Everyone in the team should know:
  - why they are in the team
  - what they are expected to deliver
  - when they are expected to deliver it
  - what resources they have at their disposal
  - how much freedom they have to work out what they should be doing.
- Make sure you understand project progress and personal contribution towards it. The team will soon learn if you don't, and progress will slacken.
- If there are problems don't wait for things to get better. Respond to performance issues, both in project progress and levels of personal contribution to the project.
- Make use of the team. Listen to their comments and feedback. Use their advice or, if you are not going to, tell them why.
- Monitor team dynamics and team politics. Respond to team and interpersonal problems that are getting in the way of the team's work.
- Even senior people are part of the team and have to come under the project manager's control. Learn how to influence more senior people to do what you require.
- Use a reasonable proportion of time managing and motivating project team members. Keep the project team motivated by:

- Setting the project team's expectations as to what it will be like to work on the project. If it will be chaotic and hard, tell them in advance.
- Explaining the importance of the project and receiving suitable feedback from senior managers.
- Ensuring the team has a clear idea about objectives and personal responsibilities.
- Keeping everyone updated on status.
- Feeding back on progress, so the team knows how the project is supported.
- Aligning performance management and annual appraisal process to performance on the project.
- Aligning project with personal needs, e.g. learning skills, being seen.
- Removing individual distractions, irritations and concerns – typical ones include:
  - not feeling that they are adding value
  - not knowing their personal work is valued
  - not knowing that their career is progressing while on the project
  - being unsure if they have a job role to go back to once the project is complete
  - avoiding demotivation: factors such as uncertainty or lack of value will create demotivations.
- Don't forget anyone in the team, especially geographically or physically separated staff. If they are working on the project, they are part of the team and need the same level of management.
- Thank or reward people for contributions appropriately.

Identifying and benefiting from quick wins

A quick win is an improvement that is visible, has benefit and is popular, that can be delivered quickly after the project starts. The quick win does not have to be profound or have a long-term impact on your organisation, but needs to be something that you can talk about and people will agree is a good thing. The best quick wins are easy and cheap to implement, and create positive discussion about the project.

1   Make sure everyone in the project team understands the benefits and importance of quick wins to a project.

2   Identify quick wins. There are many ways to identify quick wins, such as:
   - brainstorming with your core team
   - observing daily work in the organisation and listening to staff
   - asking stakeholders
   - being open to staff suggestions.

3   Review the impact of each quick win. They must have a positive, even if intangible, value. If they have any negative impact or high cost they are almost certainly not worth pursuing.

4   Determine which quick wins you will implement.

5   Thank team members for every suggestion, and tell them if you are going to implement it or not. If you do not implement the idea try to tell people why. Doing this keeps people interested.

6   Quick wins will form part of your plan of work, and once you have your work approved, implement them.

7   Make sure every relevant team and individual is aware of the benefits you have quickly achieved. Quick wins will achieve little if they are not widely communicated.

8   Cease communications after a period of time. Communicate loudly about your quick wins, but don't communicate about them for ever. Quick wins are refreshing and beneficial, but can also start to sound stale after a while.

Managing third parties on projects

Not all tasks on projects will be completed by your own staff. Some activities may be completed by third parties. This can be a major component of project management and this checklist provides only very high-level guidance.

1 Identify and scope the work required by the third party.

2 Agree who will negotiate the supplier contract, and who will manage the supplier relationship in life (the procurement department or the project team?).

3 Understand any organisation standards you have to comply with for this type of contract.

4 Determine structure of contract required. Consider:

   - Fixed price, time and materials, partnering and shared risk and reward, etc.

   - Do you want the third party to provide some resources, produce deliverables, achieve an outcome or reduce risk? These have significant bearings on the type of contract and the price.

   - Will the work be completely outsourced, or partially, or are they providing resources under your management control?

   - Is the contract for this project alone or is it part of a larger contract? Does it just include help on the project or does it need to include maintenance, support or other services?

   - How will project change and scope control be handled? This is critically important. A high percentage of contractual disputes are to do with handling changes to scope or requirements.

   - How will disputes be resolved without the overhead of escalation?

   - How will the payment schedule be linked to delivery and performance?

   - What are your handover needs – consider training, documentation and in-life support.

   - How much time do you have to put a contract in place? Are you in a hurry or do you have the time to optimise your choice?

5 Determine your selection criteria. How are you going to determine the best supplier for you? Price is usually important, but in the longer run the quality of the supplier's work is usually more important and provides greater value.

6 Determine how you will judge the quality of the third party's output or deliverables, and how you will accept or hand over deliverables. This should include any training or information the third party needs to provide you with.

7 Choose a third party to do the work.

8 Put a contract in place. The contract provides a structure to manage and a fallback if things go wrong. Day-to-day management should not continually refer to the contract.

9 Explain to your own staff why you are working with a third party. Sometimes staff can be uncomfortable when third parties are used, or can feel under-valued. Be open so that future problems can be avoided.

10 Define the way you will manage the third party, which will depend on:
   - Whether day-to-day work by the third party is visible or invisible to you – i.e. is there a tangible output you can track, or do you depend on what they say?
   - Whether you trust the third party, and have experience to base this trust upon.
   - Whether you understand the third party's performance drivers and can align your needs with their performance success.
   - Where the third party is based. Are they local or offshore?
   - Who will act as the primary interface to this supplier?
   - The degree of risk the third party is bearing on your behalf.

11 Initiate work and actively manage with regular progress updates.

12 Include the third party's work in risk management. Consider what happens if they fail to deliver, are late or the price increases. How will you avoid this? How will you mitigate against this happening?

13 Ensure complete handover. Once the supplier has completed and has been paid you may have limited opportunity for further support.

Dealing with problems – when and how to change project team members, and when to stop a project

Unfortunately, there are occasions when someone needs to be replaced on a project team.

- Before removing anyone, ascertain that they really are the cause of project problems or that the project will improve without them – do not assume this.

- Do not leave it too late. Your primary responsibility is to deliver the project, not to be nice to team members or avoid an uncomfortable situation.

- Make your decision based on the needs of the project, e.g. if the project needs intense effort, the team members need to be willing to work intensely; if they are not, then they are the wrong people for this project irrespective of other qualities.

- Check you have someone to replace the individual with. Some team members are so destructive that the team is better off without them even if there is no replacement, but on other occasions a poor performer is better than no one.

- Remember that judgements of suitability are not purely a function of personal performance, but also depend on the individual's impact on the project team. A high-performer who disrupts the project team is as much a problem as a low-performer who does not.

brilliant   tip

Before removing anyone who has worked hard on a project you should check:

- Does the poorly performing individual understand what is required of them?

- Do they understand that they are performing poorly? Will some constructive feedback resolve the issue?

- Do you understand what is driving the poor performance? Can any of these reasons be easily resolved?

- Is the individual willing and able to overcome the performance issue?

After someone has been removed from a project it will impact on their performance assessments. It is important to differentiate between poor performance, changing needs and choice of wrong person. If changing project team members is not enough, the project may need to be stopped. A project should be stopped when:

- The project is unrecoverable and will not deliver. Don't go on hoping for things to get better – if it has been bad for a long time, it is likely to continue to be so.
- The actual cost yet to be invested or spent is greater than the benefits.
- The opportunity cost of continuing is higher than the possible benefits.
- The situation in a business changes to such an extent that the project is irrelevant or the benefits the project will deliver decline below the remaining cost to deliver.

A project manager and sponsor should be brave and:

- Halt a failing project – identify if it can be realistically saved and, if not, abandon it.
- Don't wait too long for it to improve – or keep hoping that improvement is just round the corner.
- Don't overly penalise people for underperformance, unless the mistake is repeated. If the penalties are too high, people will avoid admitting mistakes and cover up problems for as long as they can.
- Even if the project is killed, try to learn from the experience and still review the project.

Signs to look out for in a failing project:

- Lack of understanding of real progress – i.e. progress is regularly worse than it should be according to reports and predictions.
- Increasing problems – such as increasing numbers of unresolved issues and increasing levels of risk.
- Increasing planning problems – work being squeezed into impossibly short periods, overly parallel working, testing and implementation cut back to unrealistically short timescales.

A strong project manager may resolve any of these issues, but they indicate major problems:

- Scope being reduced to hit targets, but to such an extent that the deliverables are no longer of value.

- No viable or believable action plan to bring the project back on track or to improve.

- Business needs change to such an extent that the project's goals are not of value to the business any more.

Reducing a project's duration

Project sponsors and project customers can place a wide variety of demands on project managers, but one of the most common is to be asked to reduce the duration of a project.

Ways to reduce a project's duration include:

- More focused management, combined with encouragement or incentives for team members to work more effectively. Managing and motivating staff to tighter timescales can reduce a project's duration.
- Faster decision making. Projects are subject to many management decisions and often have to wait for them. Faster decision making in a business may reduce project timescales.
- Adding resources can speed up the time to complete some project activities. Beware though – increased resource can speed up many projects, but it will not work in all cases and in some situations will actually slow a project down.
- Removing project constraints. Projects are subject to many constraints which can delay progress. Identify and remove them.
- Reducing the scope or quality of a project.
- Breaking a project into phases (see page 179).
- Time-boxing. Forcing completion or delivery within a set period of time creates focus in the project team on the core aspects of a project. It can be very successful, but usually has to be combined with reduced scope.
- Increasing the level of parallel working. The advantage of parallel working has to be balanced against higher risk. There are specialist approaches to parallel working such as *concurrent* or *simultaneous engineering*.
- Changing the project strategy. There are usually several ways to achieve an outcome. Review the plan or approach and look for alternative simpler or quicker ways. This can provide good results, especially if a project plan has never been reviewed.
- Stopping other projects that are getting in the way and using resources that would be more helpful on this project.

brilliant recap

Once a project is under way, the main role of the project manager is to understand progress, to manage and motivate the project team to deliver, and to regularly take decisive action to keep the project on track.

CHAPTER 8

Completing projects and implementing deliverables

As deliverables from a project are implemented and changes are made in an organisation, more staff become conscious of a project as it starts to directly affect them.

Introduction

As deliverables from a project are implemented and changes are made in an organisation, more staff become conscious of a project as it starts to directly affect them. Often, the judgement of a project's success is based on stakeholders' experience of the implementation of deliverables. How well you complete your project directly links to how successful you will be assessed to be.

If the project results in substantial change, see also Chapter 13.

Implementing deliverables

As deliverables are completed they are ready to be implemented. Implemented deliverables enable an organisation to make the transition from current ways of working to new ways – in other words, *change*. The steps in implementation are:

1   Implementation planning: implementation is complicated and risky. For a complex project a detailed implementation plan should be developed, which:

   - ensures the project's deliverables are in a fit state to be implemented
   - defines acceptance criteria and go/no-go decisions for the deliverables
   - ensures that the organisation is ready to change in the way proposed (see Chapter 13)
   - assesses the risk to the organisation from a change, and has a defined way to manage the transition
   - plans for resource to deal with unexpected problems that happen in implementation
   - contains appropriate contingency plans for go-live should anything go wrong and disrupt operations.

2   Testing and acceptance. Testing is performed to ensure the deliverables created by the project meet the need as defined in the requirements. Deliverables are normally only accepted if they confirm to defined acceptance criteria (see pages 131 and 133).

3   Implementing and handover: the deliverables are put to live use in the business and handed over to operational departments (see Chapter 13). Types of implementation include:

   - *Prototype*: sample deliverables are implemented to gather feedback. They are then enhanced based on their appropriateness, effectiveness and how staff respond to them.
   - *Pilot implementation*: trying deliverables in one area of the organisation and learning from the experience. The learning is used to decide how to carry out implementation in the rest of the organisation.
   - *Phased*: gradual roll-out across the organisation.
   - *Big bang*: single once-off implementation across the organisation.

The decision on which approach should be taken depends on:

- speed of implementation required
- scale of implementation
- the level of risk associated with the implementation, and if rollback is possible
- whether or not the implementation can be broken into chunks
- the type of deliverables and the risk associated with their use
- the degree of change and likely staff response associated with implementation.

4   Responding to issues: during implementation, unforeseen problems and unexpected outcomes will arise, and staff may resist the implementation. This cannot be planned for precisely, but it is possible to identify many implementation risks. You must be prepared to handle issues as they arise during implementation. It is rarely plain sailing!

5   Closing the project: when all remaining activities in the project are completed (see pages 135 and 136).

6   Project review: perform a review to ensure future lessons are learnt from the project (see Chapter 9).

brilliant   tip

Celebrate: if a project has been a success, the project team should be thanked and motivated for future projects with a celebration. This must not be done too early, as it can remove focus and energy on completing the project.

Testing deliverables

Project deliverables should conform to their documented requirements. To ensure they do, they must be tested prior to implementation. There are many ways to test and the type of testing required depends on the deliverables. Whatever approach to testing is taken, it is only by testing that you can be confident that deliverables are as you expect them to be.

While the actual tests vary between deliverables, there are some generic questions you need to ask to test any set of deliverables:

- Is the set of deliverables complete?
- Does each deliverable work? Do the deliverables work together as expected?
- Do the deliverables integrate smoothly with existing business processes, systems, tools, etc.?
- Does each deliverable work as intended and with all the features you expected to be in it?
- Does each deliverable work to the level of service expected, meeting non-functional requirements?
- Have the deliverables been made, built or created to the level of quality that was required?
- Are there any specific acceptance criteria or processes the customer has defined – and have the deliverables met these criteria?

The sorts of tests that are possible are:

- Formal tests, usually a series of gradually more comprehensive tests that put the deliverables closer and closer to real use. Typical stages from an IT project are:
  - unit test
  - integration test
  - user acceptance test
  - systems test
  - operational pilots.

- Internal pilots: use of the deliverables in an internal environment. Ideally, this is done in such a way that the deliverables can be removed if they do not work as expected or required (removing already implemented deliverables is called *rollback*).

- Customer trials: trialling of the deliverables with customers. This is normally done for new products and services. It can be testing, or checking attitudes to product features, pricing, etc.

Decisions about what types of tests are needed should take account of:

- The type of project and deliverables.

- The level of risk associated with implementation and use of the deliverables. The higher risk associated with using the deliverables, the more thorough testing should be.

- The project constraints in terms of speed of implementation required and resource available. Time and resource for testing should have been built into the project plan from the outset of the project.

- The type of implementation (big bang or phased – see page 129). A big bang approach often requires more thorough testing than a pilot or phased implementation.

Accepting project deliverables and gaining sign-off

A key principle is that project customers decide when deliverables are good enough, not the project team. One of the most important groups of customers is those who have to use the deliverables once implemented – known as *end-users*. The customer's or end-user's representatives should sign off deliverables as acceptable.

There are several stages of sign-off possible in a project, including signing off project scope and project requirements early in the project's life. The most important sign-offs are:

- Acceptance for implementation: when operational departments sign off that deliverables can be implemented in their departments. This sign-off is based on the testing results (see page 131) and approval of the implementation plan (see page 129).

- Acceptance that implementation is complete: when customers and end-users of the deliverables sign off that they are satisfied with the implementation and the project can now end.

The primary people involved in the above sign-offs are:

- Project sponsor: he is satisfied with the project and how the risk it exposes the business to is being managed.

- Operational departments: the people and functions who have to use and live with deliverables. There will often be several operational departments involved.

- Benefits case owner: the people and functions that have to achieve the benefits associated with these deliverables.

It is helpful to define the following criteria to manage the acceptance of deliverables:

- *Acceptance criteria*: predefined criteria agreed with project customers and users. If met, customers will accept the deliverables. Acceptance criteria are usually based on the deliverables passing tests, but may include other requirements, such as having access to documents or user instructions and staff having completed training.

- *Go/no-go criteria*: predefined criteria agreed with operational departments. If met, the operating departments will agree that implementation can go ahead.

Determining when a project is complete

Ending a project is often harder than expected. There are always further activities that can be done to improve the implementation, or to increase stakeholder satisfaction. However, the project must end – the project team members will be needed to do other work, and costs must be limited or the business case will not be met. To complete a project:

1   Prepare for completion up front. Set stakeholder expectations that the project will be ending.

2   Be clear on conditions to close the project. Completion of a project should not simply occur when a point in time is reached: closure happens after the decision that the project has been completed and the deliverables are of an appropriate standard. Operational departments should be lined up to take responsibility for deliverables as soon as acceptance criteria have been met.

3   Complete closure activities:
   - Complete any outstanding activities, or ensure they are included in the handover to end-users or operational support.
   - Release human resources at the appropriate time (see page 136).
   - Thanks and celebrations. Project team members should be thanked appropriately for their contribution to the project.
   - Review stakeholder satisfaction and agree any actions required to satisfy dissatisfied stakeholders. This includes agreeing what to do with any unfulfilled requirements.
   - Perform project staff appraisals, and for non-project staff organise feedback to their line managers on their performance on the project.
   - Finalise budgets and release any money not spent. This requires ensuring that any final payments have been made to suppliers.
   - Complete any project documentation, such as handover reports and project closure approvals.
   - Perform a project review and identify lessons learnt.

4   Gain sponsor approval to close the project.

Releasing project team members

As tasks on the project plan are completed, project team members can be released. Do not do this prematurely. People should only be released from the team when:

- You are sure that they have completed all the tasks required, not simply that they have worked until a certain date specified in the plan. All the work they were meant to do must be completed.

- You have confidence you will not need them to help you further during implementation.

Projects come to an end. Don't let this just happen by accident with people drifting off as they feel appropriate:

- Prepare early for this and don't just suddenly arrive there.

- Manage expectations as to when people will be released. Project timelines will often flex a little, and original plans to let people go on one date may move as the project shifts. Manage team members' expectations as to when they will be free to go.

- Resist pressure to let critical team members go too early. The benefits from a project can be severely reduced if key people are not available throughout handover.

- Stagger the release of people. It is unusual to be able to release everyone at once, but it is also unusual to need everyone right to the end of the project.

brilliant recap

A project is a success *only* when it ends well. Successfully completing a project in a controlled and planned way, handing over quality deliverables, and meeting stakeholder needs with minimal disruption, are indications of great project management.

CHAPTER 9

Learning from projects

Reviewing a completed project provides organisations with an excellent chance to learn. In the pressure to get on, there is often a temptation to miss out a formal review. This is a waste of a valuable opportunity. This chapter also includes a project quality assurance (QA) checklist which can be used at any stage in a project.

Determining if a project is successful or not

The basis for learning is to understand whether something is successful or not – if you do not know this you cannot draw useful conclusions. Many factors and different viewpoints have to be taken into account. Determining if a project is successful should be linked to the success criteria for the project, but expectations change as projects progress and success criteria are not always adapted in line with changing expectations.

Far from being an objective fact, determining success is often a subjective judgement. Considerations in determining if a project was successful or not are:

1   Review the tangible success criteria – have they been met, and does it appear as if they will continue to be met?

2   Were the success criteria met within the constraints in terms of scope, time and money put upon the project?

3   Review the intangible success criteria – in discussion with the project sponsor: do you think they have been met? Is this consistent with other people's views?

4   Do the project sponsor, project manager and project team feel the project was a success?

5   Do the stakeholders feel the project was a success?

6   Has anything else been gained from this project? Has the organisation's ability to deliver projects improved? Has any other improvement resulted from this project?

Performing a review of a completed project

Project reviews are the basis for improvement in project performance. Individuals learn from working on projects, but it is through discussion and action that learning is maximised. All projects, from the best to the worst-performing, provide valuable opportunities to learn.

Depending on the scale of the project, there may be one or several reviews. The review should be held soon enough after the project that it is fresh in people's minds, but long enough afterwards to understand if benefits have been achieved. If there is a considerable period between achieving benefits and completion of the project, hold two separate reviews – one to review the project and the other to review benefits.

Steps to performing a project review are:

1   Identify the audience for the project review, set up a time and location and invite participants.

2   Before running the meeting, review the checklist on page 142 – and focus on real learning output. Think about how you will use the outcome from this project review, so it is not just a talking shop.

3   Introduce the review. Make sure everyone knows this is not a performance review or an opportunity to point fingers. It is a session to learn for future projects.

4   Start with a freeform debate on the project and let people express views on their experiences and feelings about the project. It is not necessary to record this debate. This enables people to get things off their chests. Try to ensure that everyone present expresses an opinion. Keep this debate to 30 minutes to 1 hour maximum.

5   Have a short coffee break. Inform everyone that, on their return, they will start a more structured review process.

6 Review whether the project was a success or not, and in what ways. Differences in opinions on success are often the basis of good learning points. Try to make this as factual as possible.

- Was the team's view of how successful the project was different from the stakeholders'?
- What can be learnt from this?

7 Go into a more structured set of questions:

- What was not done during this change that you should do in future? (Start doing this in future.)
- What went badly during this change that you should make sure you do not do in future? (Stop doing this in future.)
- What went well during this change that you should make sure you always do in future? (Continue doing this in future.)
- Is there anything else you have learnt that is worth remembering for next time?

8 Document the findings from the review. For every learning point assign a tangible action, with an action owner to ensure that it is carried forward.

Ensuring lessons are learnt

A common problem with project reviews is that they do not result in changes in behaviour or approach, so no effective learning takes place. Making sure that learning happens needs a conscious effort on behalf of project reviewers. Some questions to prompt/encourage people to learn lessons from a project are as follows:

- How will you ensure you start, stop and continue the points you note from the project review?

- How will you ensure that this learning is shared widely within the organisation, so that not only you and the project team learn, but the whole organisation does?

- Do you need to adapt or enhance any of the processes, procedures or methods used for project management in the organisation? If so, how will you communicate these to the whole organisation?

- Do you need to adapt or enhance any of the roles and responsibilities used in projects? If so, how will you do this and ensure it happens next time?

- Would your project be better supported by new systems and tools? If so, what are they and how will you ensure your organisation has access to them?

- Did anyone perform particularly well on this project? How will you ensure that this individual is rewarded and encouraged to repeat this behaviour on the next project and encourage it in others? How can you use this person's skills to teach others?

- Who is going to perform all the actions identified, and by when? Who will ensure the action is done? The actions may relate to future projects, changing existing processes or tools, or behaviours of individuals.

Improving an organisation's project performance

Improving project performance is dependent on a wide range of factors beyond simply performing project reviews. Key points are to:

1 Develop a culture in the project management team(s) which values enhancing skills and learning new approaches.

2 Perform project reviews and ensure that learning is shared.

3 Be clear about the competencies and behaviours required by project managers.

4 Have role models who are well regarded and show the behaviours and performance expected of project managers.

5 Tailor the organisation's performance management systems so that they encourage the behaviour you want from project managers.

6 Provide adequate rewards and career structure to motivate project managers to perform.

7 Build a team with the right skills, competencies and culture to meet the needs of the organisation.

8 Develop and implement the right project management tools and infrastructure, optimised for the scale and type of projects required.

9 Constantly challenge and enhance project checklists and processes as a result of project experiences.

10 Provide access to training, so that project managers can enhance their skills.

11 Provide the right range and volume of staff for projects.

12 Build a management culture that values project management and project managers, and acts in a way that is consistent with the needs of projects.

13 Study appropriate organisations and benchmark project management performance against them. Constantly review what you can learn from other situations.

14 Ensure that good governance processes exist, so not only are projects done well, but the right projects are chosen to be delivered, and the right decisions are made about projects.

Performing project or programme QA

A project quality assurance (QA) is a detailed review of a project or programme. This is longer than a project status review session. It can be done at any stage of a project or programme. At the end of the QA you should understand the status of the project, the quality of the project management process and the abilities of the project manager, and be able to identify learning opportunities and improvements to be made. A good QA will detect current issues, future risks, and information pertinent to other projects.

The following table provides an extensive list of questions. It is not expected that all of these will be asked at a QA session, but a sample may be selected depending on the status and phase of the project. An effective QA not only asks questions, but also seeks evidence for the answers.

Area of QA	Questions to ask
Scope, objectives and requirements	• Are the project's objectives understood and documented?
	• Does the project have well-understood success criteria?
	• Is the project generally being managed in a way that will meet the objectives and success criteria?
	• Does the project have defined requirements?
	• Do the requirements link back to the project objectives?
	• Are deliverables from the project defined in clear and, if appropriate, quantified terms?
	• Have the project stakeholders been identified?
	• Are the scope, objectives and requirements approved by an appropriate range of stakeholders?

→

Area of QA	Questions to ask
Business case	<ul><li>Does the project have a compelling business case?</li><li>Were the appropriate people involved in the development of the business case?</li><li>Does the business case have the appropriate level of management authorisation?</li><li>Has the business case been updated in line with any changes as the project progresses?</li><li>Does the business case take account of risk?</li></ul>
Planning and schedule management	<ul><li>Is the plan developed from a suitable project strategy and project life cycle?</li><li>Does the project have a plan which identifies all the tasks necessary to meet the objectives and produce the agreed deliverables?</li><li>Is the plan at the right level of detail to aid estimation, management of the project and task allocation?</li><li>Are project estimates accurate, and has appropriate contingency been built into the plan to account for the level of uncertainty in the estimates?</li><li>Is the plan used as an active tool and updated as the project progresses? Are variances from plan identified and addressed?</li><li>Has the project progressed to plan so far? If not, what has been done about this?</li><li>Was the plan developed taking into account the right balance of time, cost and quality constraints?</li><li>Does the plan contain appropriate milestones for senior-level reporting?</li><li>Does the plan contain a communications plan? Is there evidence of ongoing communications and expectations management?</li><li>Does the plan contain all the necessary dependencies and the right sort of dependencies?</li><li>Are resources being applied to the project tasks as planned?</li></ul>

Area of QA	Questions to ask
Resources	• Does the project have adequate resources to complete its tasks within the agreed time frames? Were these resources allocated according to the needs of the plan? • Do the project team members work effectively as a team? • Was there an appropriate mobilisation process to start the project? • Do the project team members have clear roles? • Does the project have an approved budget? • Are the operational managers who provide resource to the project committed to providing them? • Does the project have an effective project manager? • Are suppliers being used effectively? Are the right contracts in place with an appropriate control mechanism to support them?

Management processes	• Is there evidence for the following processes, with a clear definition of the process, and supporting up-to-date paperwork showing that the processes are used:
	  – risk management
	  – issue management
	  – change control
	  – assumption management
	• What are the current most significant risks and issues? What is being done about them?
	• Are assumptions actively managed and linked to risk management?
	• What has the impact of change been upon this project so far?
	• Are there appropriate contingency plans in place? Are the triggers to initiate the contingency plans well understood?
	• Does the project manager have an appropriate system of status reviews and progress reporting? Is there an associated series of reports to key stakeholders?
	• Does the project manager perform regular stakeholder management?
	• Has the project manager encouraged communication across the project team? Is it working?
	• Does the project have an appropriate administrative process, including document management?

→

Area of QA	Questions to ask
Delivery and implementation	• Is there an appropriate implementation plan? • Has sufficient, structured testing been built into the project plan? • Is there sufficient time for a quality implementation? • Do operational departments accept their role in the project handover? • Has the implementation been planned and managed as an effective change? • Were all the appropriate functions ready and prepared for implementation? • Were resources released from the project in a controlled way and at the most appropriate time?
Benefits	• Is the project being managed to optimise benefits? • Are processes in place to track benefits? • Will the project meet its business case? • Who is responsible for achieving benefits? Do they accept this responsibility?
Project close-down	• Was the project a success? How was this determined? • Has a project review been arranged? • Have lessons been learnt from this project? • Have the lessons been applied in practice? How? What has changed as a result? • Was there an appropriate celebration of project completion?
Governance	• Does the project exist within the organisation's project portfolio? • Is the project approved and prioritised? • Does the project have a sponsor of sufficient seniority, who allocates an appropriate amount of time to supporting this project? • Does the sponsor respond effectively to escalations for help or decisions? • Is the project supported by timely management decision making and approvals?
Quality	• Are project processes in line with the organisation's standards? If not, is any variance reasonable and justifiable? • Do the project's deliverables have defined quality metrics to conform to? Do they conform?

brilliant recap

The organisations with the best track records in project management treat every project as an opportunity to learn and improve. They put formal processes in place to ensure this happens.

CHAPTER 10

Core project management tools and processes

Project management provides a wide selection of tools for different situations. Among these are several core management tools and processes used throughout all projects. This chapter provides advice on the core tools, and overviews the wider set of tools available.

Risk management process checklist

This checklist shows whether your risk management process is complete. For any question you answer 'no' to, decide how to include it in your risk management process.

Risk management process questions	Yes	No
Do you have a process for capturing risks that all members of your project team are aware of and are using?	☐	☐
Do you understand all of the factors that are causing risk to your project, or by your project upon your organisation?	☐	☐
Have you documented every risk in a common risk log?	☐	☐
Have you captured the key information about your risks, including: ● Description ● When captured ● Impact and likelihood ● Owner ● Action required to resolve ● Resolution due by	☐ ☐ ☐ ☐ ☐ ☐	☐ ☐ ☐ ☐ ☐ ☐
Do you need to perform quantitative risk assessment as well as qualitative – and do you know how to?	☐	☐
Does every risk have an owner who understands the actions they are responsible for to manage the risk?	☐	☐
Are you tracking and managing the resolution of risks?	☐	☐
Do you regularly review risks?	☐	☐
Have you escalated any key risks to your sponsor and other customers?	☐	☐
When risks are identified and actions for resolution assigned to a named owner, are they generally resolved?	☐	☐
Are you tracking the trend in risks in your project to ensure it is not going out of control, e.g.: ● cumulative risk profile for the project (increasing, decreasing or staying stable) ● amount of resource used in resolving unplanned risks (increasing, decreasing or staying stable)?	 ☐ ☐	 ☐ ☐

The sources of risk

The following checklist will help in identifying your project's risks. It does not tell you what your risks are, but will help to trigger your thinking. For every question to which you answer 'no', consider the possible risk implications. It is not possible to write a generic set of risks that is exhaustive, and so this should be used as a starting point for identifying risk, rather than for understanding your full risk situation.

	Yes	No	N/A	So the risk is ...
Project definition:				
● Are the objectives clear and unambiguous?	☐	☐	☐	_____
● Is the scope clear and fully understood?	☐	☐	☐	_____
● Are the requirements clear and fully understood?	☐	☐	☐	_____
● Are targets clear and fully understood?	☐	☐	☐	_____
● Do you know how you will achieve your project's objectives? If not, do you have a way to achieve this understanding?	☐	☐	☐	_____
Business case and budget:				
● Are your project's budget and cost estimate robust?	☐	☐	☐	_____
● Is your business case robust?	☐	☐	☐	_____
● Is the business case based on valid and reasonable assumptions?	☐	☐	☐	_____
● Are the business case sensitivities understood?	☐	☐	☐	_____

→

	Yes	No	N/A	So the risk is . . .
Support for the project:				
● Does the business accept the project's objectives?	☐	☐	☐	_____
● Does the business accept the proposed solution?	☐	☐	☐	_____
● Does the project have adequate prioritisation?	☐	☐	☐	_____
● Is there sufficient active sponsorship and management support?	☐	☐	☐	_____
● Are management responsibilities and accountabilities stable and unlikely to change? (Are your key sponsors liable to stay your key sponsors?)	☐	☐	☐	_____
● Do your sponsor and customers understand the level of risk in the project and accept this?	☐	☐	☐	_____
Expectations:				
● Are expectations about the project reasonable?	☐	☐	☐	_____
● Are expectations manageable?	☐	☐	☐	_____
Plan:				
● Is your plan complete? Are you confident that you have missed nothing out?	☐	☐	☐	_____
● Are you confident that your estimates of task length and resource requirement are correct?	☐	☐	☐	_____
● Are you confident that your schedule of tasks is correct, and that it reflects the impact of dependencies?	☐	☐	☐	_____
● Do you have sufficient contingency in your plan and budget to overcome any risks that may occur?	☐	☐	☐	_____

→

	Yes	No	N/A	So the risk is . . .
Resources:				
● Do you have sufficient resources to complete your project?	☐	☐	☐	_____
● Do the resources have the necessary skills and capabilities?	☐	☐	☐	_____
● Are the resources available?	☐	☐	☐	_____
● Will the resources continue to be available?	☐	☐	☐	_____
● Are all key and scarce resources that you cannot afford to lose and that would be difficult to replace guaranteed for the whole project?	☐	☐	☐	_____
● Are the team motivated to do the task?	☐	☐	☐	_____
● For any third-party suppliers – do you have a good relationship and workable contract?	☐	☐	☐	_____
Project management:				
● Do you have a good project manager with the capability to deliver a project of this nature? (The project manager can be a source of risk.)	☐	☐	☐	_____
● Do you have access to a good range of project management tools, processes and documentation?	☐	☐	☐	_____
Assumptions:				
● Do you know all the key assumptions made in this project?	☐	☐	☐	_____
● Do you understand the risk associated with each of these assumptions?	☐	☐	☐	_____

→

	Yes	No	N/A	So the risk is . . .
Change:				
● Is the project stable and not subject to regular change?	☐	☐	☐	_____
● Do you have a robust process for managing change?	☐	☐	☐	_____
● If there is change, is it change at a rate you can manage?	☐	☐	☐	_____
Issues:				
● Do you have a robust process for managing issues?	☐	☐	☐	_____
● Are any issues arising occurring at a rate you can manage and not getting out of control?	☐	☐	☐	_____
Stakeholder management:				
● Do you know who your stakeholders are, what their views of the project are, and do you have a way to manage or use them?	☐	☐	☐	_____
● Are your stakeholders free of issues that add risk to your project?	☐	☐	☐	_____
Communications:				
● Do you have access to all the information you need?	☐	☐	☐	_____
● Do you understand the information needs of your different audiences?	☐	☐	☐	_____
● Do you have access to all the necessary communication channels?	☐	☐	☐	_____

→

	Yes	No	N/A	So the risk is . . .
Suppliers:				
● Do you know who you will use?	☐	☐	☐	_____
● If you need to go through a selection and contracting process are the time and resource for this built into the plan?	☐	☐	☐	_____
● Does the supplier have the skills and resources available to do the work you require them to do?	☐	☐	☐	_____
● Do you have the right contract with your suppliers?	☐	☐	☐	_____
● Do you have the right relationship with your suppliers?	☐	☐	☐	_____
Effective management and governance:				
● Do you have an effective way to escalate issues?	☐	☐	☐	_____
● Do you have an effective decision-making process?	☐	☐	☐	_____
● Are timelines for business decisions and approvals built into your plan?	☐	☐	☐	_____
Impact of other projects or programmes:				
● Is there any risk of resources being moved to other projects or programmes?	☐	☐	☐	_____
● Do you understand your dependencies on other projects or programmes?	☐	☐	☐	_____
● Are you confident these will be delivered on time?	☐	☐	☐	_____
● Are you in control of, or have reliable commitments for, anything else in your business that could impact on your project?	☐	☐	☐	_____

→

	Yes	No	N/A	So the risk is . . .
Business impact and readiness for change:				
• Is the business capable of absorbing or handling the change you propose in the light of everything else done?	☐	☐	☐	_____
• Do you understand the impact on staff of the project?	☐	☐	☐	_____
• Do you understand the impact on management of the project?	☐	☐	☐	_____
• Do you understand the impact on suppliers of the project?	☐	☐	☐	_____
• Do you understand the impact on customers of the project?	☐	☐	☐	_____
• Are customers ready for the change and any work they have to do to support the project being implemented (e.g. testing, training)?	☐	☐	☐	_____
• Do you understand the impact on any other key stakeholder group?	☐	☐	☐	_____
• Have you got a robust way to understand and manage these impacts?	☐	☐	☐	_____
• Is the risk on the business manageable in case the project does not deliver?	☐	☐	☐	_____
• Is the risk on the business manageable in case any aspect of the project goes wrong?	☐	☐	☐	_____
• Is the risk on the business manageable in case the project delivers, but disrupts the business?	☐	☐	☐	_____
Familiarity with project:				
• Are you generally familiar with your project and do you have experience of projects of this nature? Does your project have any unique or novel aspects?	☐	☐	☐	_____

Dealing with risks

Use this checklist when you have identified your risks and need help in understanding the implications. It contains a summary of qualitative risk assessment. (Quantitative risk assessment is outside of the scope of this book.)

1   Do you understand what the risk is?
    - What will this risk affect if it occurs, the project or the business? (In the worst case will the risk make the project fail, or will it have wider implications for your business or organisation?)
    - Is it a project risk? Can you manage it, with your sponsor's and customers' support?
    - Is it a business risk? Make sure the parts of the business affected by the risk understand and accept the risk.

2   Define a scale on which you will assess impact and likelihood of risk. For small projects a simple scale of high, medium and low is usually enough.

3   What is the impact on the project of this risk occurring?

4   What is the likelihood of the risk occurring?

5   What is the impact on the business or organisation if this risk occurs? Overall risk = likelihood × impact.

Use the following checklist to decide on the appropriate management action when you have identified and assessed the risk.

1   Start risk management as your project begins. When you start thinking about the project and developing your plan, think about risk. The best way to deal with risks is to identify them early and build any action to overcome them into your plan.

2   Don't worry when you find risks – project management is largely about risk management!

3   Put a risk management process in place (see page 151).

4   Identify risks (see page 152).

5   Understand and prioritise risks (see above).

6 Ensure stakeholders and customers understand project risks.

7 Decide on action for each prioritised risk:

- Do nothing, but continue to monitor.
- Reduce the likelihood of the risk occurring.
- Reduce the project's exposure to the risk.
- Make a contingency plan to deal with the effects of the risk.
- In the worst case, if the risk to business is too high and it is not possible to mitigate or avoid the risk, stop the project and determine if there is a different way to achieve your goals.

8 Determine the most appropriate time to take action. It may be now; it may be later when a specific event has occurred or you have more information. (However, you have to do it soon enough so that your action will be effective.)

9 Take the risk management action.

10 Assess the result and, if necessary, keep taking action.

11 Continue to manage risks throughout the life of the project.

Dealing with issues

Problems will arise on projects. Any problem that disrupts the project is known as an *issue*. The following list provides a set of questions to help in identifying issues. For any question to which you answer 'yes', you may have an issue.

	Yes	No
Do you have any uncertainty or ambiguity in understanding what an issue is?	☐	☐
Are there any issues causing delay to your project or any of the activities in it?	☐	☐
Are there any issues causing increased cost to your project?	☐	☐
Do you have any issues as the project manager, which impact on your ability to perform your job effectively?	☐	☐
Are there any issues causing concerns or problems for your project team?	☐	☐
Are there any difficulties or problems with accessing any of the resources you need for the project?	☐	☐
Are there any issues causing problems in the completion of any activity in your project?	☐	☐
Are there any issues causing problems with the quality, scope or completeness of your deliverables?	☐	☐
Are there any problems in defining the requirements for your project?	☐	☐
Are there any issues affecting the project sponsor, or her ability to perform an effective sponsorship role?	☐	☐
Are there any issues affecting your stakeholders, stakeholder expectations or their judgements of project success?	☐	☐
Are there any issues affecting the way you will test and implement the project's deliverables?	☐	☐
Are there any issues affecting the capability of this project to deliver business benefits or meet the project's business case?	☐	☐

→

	Yes	No
Are there any problems related to project management standards or processes in use within your organisation?	☐	☐
Are there any issues regarding the governance processes in your organisation, and how decisions or approvals regarding your project are made?	☐	☐

The next checklist gives you guidance as to whether your issue management process is complete. For any question you answer 'no' to, think through the implications and decide how to include this in your process.

Issue management process questions	Yes	No
Do you have a process for capturing issues that all members of your project team are aware of and are using?	☐	☐
Do you understand all the factors that are causing delay, additional spend or increased risk on your project?	☐	☐
Have you documented every issue in a project issues log?	☐	☐
Is what you have documented really the root cause or only a symptom of your issue?	☐	☐
Have you captured the key information about your issues, including: • description • when captured • owner • action required to resolve • resolution due by?	☐ ☐ ☐ ☐ ☐	☐ ☐ ☐ ☐ ☐
Is your list of issues complete?	☐	☐
Does every issue have an owner who understands the actions they are responsible for to resolve the issue?	☐	☐
Are you tracking and managing the resolution of issues?	☐	☐
Do you regularly review issues?	☐	☐
Have you escalated any key issues to your sponsor and other customers?	☐	☐

→

	Yes	No
When issues are identified and actions for resolution assigned to a named owner, are they generally resolved?	☐	☐
Are you tracking the trend in issues in your project to ensure it is not going out of control, e.g.:		
• time to resolve issues (increasing, decreasing or staying stable)	☐	☐
• total number of issues (increasing, decreasing or staying stable)	☐	☐
• amount of resource used in resolving unplanned issues (increasing, decreasing or staying stable).	☐	☐

Dealing with assumptions

Assumptions are a source of risk on projects, yet assumptions must be made. There is nothing wrong with making assumptions, as long as they are explicit and reasonable. Unfortunately, assumptions are often implicit or unconscious, and difficult to identify. To detect assumptions:

1 Constantly identify assumptions:

- As you consolidate or create project information such as scoping documents and project plans.
- Through assumption review sessions. Pull together the project team specifically to review the project plan, scope, requirements, etc. for assumptions.
- Through feedback from reviewers, the project sponsor and stakeholders. They will often identify assumptions.
- As an ongoing part of the project. All team members should be able to notify the project manager of new assumptions.

2 In each situation ask: is there a factual and logical basis for the information I am using, or the decisions I am making? If not, you are making an assumption. Are there any jumps in my logic? If there are, you may be making an assumption.

3 Clarify and verify any assumptions you are making:

- What is the assumption? Document it and remove any ambiguity from the definition.
- Check it is reasonable to make an assumption. Do you have to make an assumption – i.e., is there no factual information available, or is the cost or effort of getting that information higher than is reasonable?
- Is this the most reasonable assumption you can make at this time?

4 Filter out irrelevant assumptions – those that are trivial (e.g., I assume there will be paper in the photocopier when I get there) and those which common sense dictates should be ignored (e.g., we assume the company we are working for will still exist tomorrow).

Assumptions should be managed. The following steps provide a straightforward way to manage assumptions:

5 Identify and log the assumption. You must get into the habit of documenting assumptions. A common shared assumptions log visible to and accessible by the whole project team is the best way to do this.

6 Identify the sensitivity of the project to the assumption. What will happen if this assumption is false?

7 Assess the likelihood of the assumption being false.

8 Update the risk register accordingly, and put any risk management activities in place if the assumption has a high impact or high probability of being wrong.

9 Assign an assumption owner – responsible for tracking the assumption and alerting the project manager if it changes.

10 Challenge each assumption – ensure it is reasonable. Ask yourself questions such as:

   - Do you really have to make an assumption?
   - Is the assumption you have made reasonable?
   - In what conditions is it true?
   - Can those conditions be removed?

11 If appropriate, set a date for the assumption to be verified by.

12 Verify assumptions, and as you do update the project and the plan according to the facts.

Change control

Change control is a critical process in project management, providing a process to manage the implementation of changes. Modifications or alterations will always occur on projects, and without change control projects risk descending into chaos. Change control should not stop the project altering, but makes sure it is done in a controlled way.

Change control is conceptually simple:

1   Document the proposed change in sufficient detail for the change to be clear and unambiguous.

2   Justify the change: describe why the change is being proposed, and the benefits of implementing the change.

3   Identify when the change needs to be accepted by, if it is to be effective.

4   Identify the impact of the change – will it alter the length of the project, the resources required, or the cost? Does it change the level of quality or risk? Will it affect assessments of project success?

5   Seek authorisation for the change, accepting the impact on the project. Authorisation comes from the project sponsor and key stakeholders.

6   Note the proposed action with regard to this change. The action can be: accept and implement the change, modify the request, or reject it.

7   Keep track of the current status of the change. It can be:
   - 'in review', i.e. the change is currently being assessed
   - 'accepted', i.e. it is agreed and has been built into plans
   - 'rejected', i.e. the project will continue unchanged
   - 'closed', i.e. the change has been actioned.

8   Implement any agreed actions regarding the change.

9   Monitor the impact of the change and, if appropriate, take remedial action following the implementation of a change.

Project managers and sponsors must consider the cumulative impact of changes on the project. If there are too many changes, the project becomes unstable and it becomes difficult to deliver. *Scope creep* is the name for a situation in which the cumulative impact of many changes risks the project becoming unachievable, or the project bearing no resemblance to the original objectives.

Identifying and managing stakeholders

Successful project teams interact with a wide range of people who will be impacted by the project and who have an impact on the project. These are the project stakeholders. Project stakeholders are identified in order to understand and collect requirements, to determine project success criteria, and because they are an integral part of any change following project completion.

1   Identify the stakeholders in the project:

- Who will benefit from the project?
- Who will suffer from the project?
- Who else is interested in the project?
- Think about internal customers, internal suppliers, users, financiers, staff and anyone else who will benefit or lose from the project. For some projects you should consider stakeholders external to the firm (customers, trade unions, suppliers).

2   Review the set of potential stakeholders with the project sponsor. Amend list accordingly.

3   Assess the power, influence, attitude towards the project and openness to change of each of the stakeholders:

- Power or influence: how capable is each of the stakeholders of disrupting or helping this project?
- Attitude: how likely is each of the stakeholders to help or disrupt the project?
- Openness to change: people with fixed ideas can be powerful supporters but difficult objectors.

4   Categorise the groups of stakeholders:

- High power and influence + positive attitude to the project: try to get them actively supporting the project and working to overcome any resisters.
- High power and influence + negative attitude to the project: try to overcome their objections. If this is not possible, use your supporters to block their influence.

- Low power and influence + positive attitude to the project: try to choose your project team from this group.
- Low power and influence + negative attitude to the project: use general communications and presentations to try and convince them.

5   Identify which stakeholders and groups of stakeholders you will actively manage as part of the project. Concentrate on those stakeholders with the strongest positive or negative views on the project or abilities to influence project outcomes – and those stakeholders you are capable of managing or influencing.

6   Determine how to utilise the various stakeholder groups that you will manage.

7   Build stakeholder needs into project activity plan, especially the communications plan. (See pages 89 and 98).

8   Periodically review stakeholders' views. Attitudes can change as projects progress, and the variety of stakeholders can also evolve as the project impacts on different people.

A key part of stakeholder management is *expectations management*. This involves communications to ensure that stakeholder expectations are in line with what the project will deliver. By managing expectations, project managers avoid many problems. Key points about expectations management are:

- Understand that expectations management is an important task. Although it may not directly affect delivery, it has a significant impact on the interpretation of project success.
- Start managing expectations from the very beginning of the project.
- Regularly communicate with all key stakeholders. Explore their expectations and try to influence them to be in line with the reality of the project.
- Always try to under-promise and over-deliver.
- Try to avoid surprises on the project – surprises indicate you are either not in control or you are not telling the full truth. Either will lead to reduced trust and negative expectations.

Estimating and managing a project budget

A budget must be agreed at the initiation of a project to provide the funds for the project. (Also see pages 89 and 235.)

1 Identify what components of the project must be paid for. There are many items which are obvious, such as the resources to be bought for the project. For some items it is less clear whether they have to be budgeted for or not. If you are unclear discuss with your finance department. For example:

- Staff time – is this charged for? If so, at what rate and how is it tracked?
- Internal facilities and consumables, e.g. meeting rooms and printing facilities.
- Indirect cost allocations. Is a percentage of indirect costs added to the project (e.g. overhead, and general and administrative costs)?
- Capital investments made by the project.
- In-life and operational costs once the project has gone live. These are usually picked up in operational budgets, but sometimes a project is expected to pay them for a certain period, e.g. until the end of the current financial year.

2 Based on the project plan, determine how much of each resource must be paid for.

3 Add contingency. The percentage of contingency should be related to the level of risk in the project.

4 Create a draft budget.

5 Have the draft budget reviewed by the project sponsor and the finance department. Update according to feedback.

6 Determine if the project is already budgeted for or not in an operational or line manager's budget:

- If it is budgeted for, ensure that the allocated budget matches what the project requires.
- If it is not budgeted for, determine where the project budget will be allocated from.

7 Seek approval for the budget, using normal approval processes.

8 Amend budget and project plan according to approval. If less is approved than required, the project strategy or scope needs to be reviewed.

9 Track usage, e.g. even if a bill has not been raised, you have effectively spent money as soon as you have committed to using a resource.

10 Track progress against the budget. The aim is for the budget to decline at no faster rate than progress is being made (taking account of exceptional purchases). (See page 107.)

11 Seek approval for additional spend or to access contingency funds if required.

12 Release any funds remaining at the end of project.

Other considerations when planning or managing a project budget are:

- The effects of an organisation's financial reporting cycles.

- The ways in which finance departments track expenditure and progress, which may be quite different from the way in which project managers track them.

- Approval processes to spend money within a budget. Although a total budget is approved, individual items of significant expenditure may still require approval.

- The accounting treatments and the associated implications for different types of budget categories (e.g. opex (operating costs) and capex (capital costs)).

- Handling multiple budgets and the need to allocate project costs across different cost centres.

- Accounting practice in terms of what is and what is not expected to be accounted for in a project.

- Purchase requisition (PR) and purchase order (PO) processes, and the associated approval timeframes.

Project performance metrics

There is a wide range of performance metrics to assess projects. This list provides a sample of them. Metrics are used to support the management of an individual project and to compare projects. Whichever metrics are used, care should be taken to ensure that sources of data are accurate. While performance can be indicated by a metric, it usually requires interpretation and contextual information.

There are three types of measures to assess project performance:

● measures which quantify project progress, e.g. 60 per cent of project tasks are complete

● measures which quantify delivery, e.g. 60 per cent of project deliverables have been created

● measures which quantify outcomes, e.g. 60 per cent of expected benefits have been achieved.

Potential metrics for comparison between projects or assessing overall performance are:

● delivery to time and cost

● percentage of expected benefits delivered

● return on project investment

● stakeholder satisfaction levels

● staff satisfaction and staff assessment of learning from project.

For the management of a project:

● performance at a point in time:
  – progress versus plan
  – number of open issues
  – number of open risks
  – cumulative risk level (if using quantitative risk assessments)
  – number of change controls raised

- schedule variance and cost variance (if using EVA – Earned Value Analysis)
- percentage of expected benefits delivered.
- Progress trends:
  - activity completed versus planned
  - actual spend versus planned spend
  - percentage contingency use versus percentage complete
  - number of open issues over time
  - number of risks over time
  - number of change controls over time
  - cumulative risk level over time (if using quantitative risk assessments)
  - schedule variance and cost variance over time (if using EVA)
  - progress towards overall benefits targets.

Additional and more advanced project management techniques and tools

A book of checklists is a reduced version of the richness and variety of project management approaches. This table contains references to more advanced project management techniques.

Additional techniques and tools	Why
Alternative life cycles and rapid development approaches (e.g. iterative approaches, Agile, concurrent engineering, critical chain, goal-directed project management)	• Reduce project duration • Different type of project from those you are used to
Bodies of Knowledge (e.g. APM BoK, PM BoK)	• Broad reference sources for project management techniques and tools. A rich body of knowledge about projects and project management
Change management	• Organisational change • Minimise the operational risk • Maximise the likelihood of achieving sustained change
Contract types for project suppliers (e.g. fixed price, time and materials, shared risk-reward, partnering)	• Third-party suppliers • Outsourced projects • Various contract types provide different ways of control. Each is suitable for different situations
Control and progress assessment (e.g. Earned Value Analysis (EVA), or Earned Schedule)	• To track project progress combining both progress to schedule and progress against budget

Additional techniques and tools	Why
Creative approaches (e.g. brainstorming, Delphi technique, storyboarding, facilitation approaches)	• Identification of project concepts and solutions to overcome problems • Understanding project tasks to develop a project plan • Issue and risk identification • Overcoming roadblocks or problems • Developing contingency plans
Critical chain	• When applying the Critical Chain method or CCPM
Critical path	• To identify the set of tasks that create the length of a project, and which, if delayed, will increase the project's duration
Estimation techniques (e.g. PERT)	• You cannot estimate the project with accuracy, and there is a risk in your estimates
Financial formulae (e.g. NPV, IRR) and data (e.g. discount rates)	• Business case development and prioritisation
Financial management approaches	• Complex budgets • Project requires more advanced financial management • Tools for assessing project portfolios, e.g. real options
Maturity models (e.g. OPM3, CMMI, P2MM)	• To benchmark and improve project management capability
Project crashing	• To reduce project duration, when willing to add resources
Proprietary or standardised project management or programme management approaches (e.g. Prince 2, MSP)	• Where methodologies are mandated or where you do not have existing project management standards. Increasingly such methods are industry standards and some level of expertise in them is important for all project managers

→

Additional techniques and tools	Why
Quantitative risk assessment techniques (e.g. sensitivity analysis, probabilistic such as Monte Carlo assessments)	• When qualitative risk assessment is not sufficient • To understand absolute risk levels • To determine cumulative risk levels
Requirements collection and business analysis techniques	• Complex or non-trivial requirements • Uncertainty and ambiguity in requirements
Resource management techniques (e.g. resource levelling, resource smoothing)	• You want to level the rate of resource use, or to manage resources across multiple projects
Value engineering	• To improve the design of, and maximise the value of, deliverables
Value management	• To maximise the value an organisation receives from a project investment

brilliant recap

Project management provides a very wide range of tools and processes. All project managers understand the core tools and processes. The best project managers are familiar with a broader set of tools and techniques, and tailor their use to the needs of the individual project.

PART 3

Managing
multiple projects

This part provides tips and tools to manage multiple projects. Multiple projects can be structured as a programme, or may be part of a portfolio of projects and programmes.

In addition, this part provides advice on setting up and running a project management team.

This part of the book is split into two chapters:

11 **Multiple projects** – managing multiple projects.

12 **Managing a project management team** – setting up and running a project management team.

CHAPTER 11

Multiple projects

Chapter 11 contains checklists for
managing multiple projects and
programmes, and introduces portfolio
management.

When to break a project into phases

Sometimes it is helpful to break projects into smaller chunks, called *phases*, and to manage delivery by phase or *sub-project*.

Phases should be logically coherent pieces of work. They may have dependencies on other phases, but it should make sense to manage them independently. Breaking a project into phases can reduce risk and complexity, but too many phases can make it difficult to bring them back to one coherent outcome.

There are various possible reasons for breaking a project into phases, including:

- Delivering the project in one phase has high complexity or risk. Individual phases, which can be scoped and managed one at a time, are more straightforward.
- A project is not approved because of investment limits, but an individual phase is, since the phase investment is within thresholds. Be careful doing this, as it can create problems with business cases, especially when benefits are achieved only when all phases are complete.
- There are not enough resources to deliver the whole project, or with current resources it will take an extended period of time. By breaking it into phases, the existing resources can at least deliver some of the project quickly.
- Project requirements are unclear or very volatile, and achieving clarity and completeness will take an extended period of time. A subset of the requirements is clear and this can be delivered without waiting for all requirements to be specified.
- Different parts of the project will be delivered by unrelated teams, which can work separately.
- A single project will take a long time to deliver, delaying achievement of business benefits. If a proportion of benefits can be delivered earlier, then break it into phases.

Projects can be divided into different types of phases:

- sequential
- overlapping
- parallel.

The choice of phasing depends on the context and the reason for breaking a project into phases. If the reason is resource constraints, the phases have to be sequential.

Programmes

When a project is broken into several chunks which are projects in their own right, the resulting set of projects is usually known as a *programme*. The term 'programme' refers to several different types of endeavours, including:

- Large projects – not really a helpful definition, but many people who manage large projects refer to them as programmes.
- A sequential chain of related projects, e.g. different phases of implementation of an IT system.
- A set of connected projects with a common goal, e.g. a cost-reduction programme.
- An initiative which leads to substantial organisation change, e.g. a reorganisation programme.
- A series of projects completed for a common customer within a business, e.g. a sales improvement programme.
- A complex activity that has both project and operational components, e.g. a build–operate–transfer programme for a new power station.

The use of the term depends on the situation, and usually it is not necessary to be prescriptive. In this book, a programme is assumed to contain multiple projects.

Core programme management tasks

The majority of programme management tasks are the same as for project management, although they tend to be on a larger scale. There are some tasks which are more common in programme management and are unlikely to be required in a project, including:

- Initiating projects and selecting project managers.
- Coordination between projects, e.g. dependency management.
- Consolidation of management information across projects, e.g. issues, risks, progress, reporting, etc.
- Prioritisation and resource management between projects.
- Multiple-project management and aligning multiple projects to a common goal.
- Ability to lead, motivate and direct multiple project managers.

Additionally, there are tasks which are not unique to programmes, but which tend to become more important and involved in programme management, including:

- Benefits realisation.
- Change management and managing the business acceptance of change.
- Stakeholder management involving wider and more senior stakeholder groups.
- Communications.
- Financial management.
- Understanding of interactions between programme and business governance.

Choosing a programme manager

The programme manager has to do everything a project manager does, but at a more senior level. The programme manager therefore has to have:

- Project/programme management knowledge and experience, suitable to a programme of this type and scale.
- Context-specific knowledge – both of the type of programme and of the type of organisation.
- Personal capabilities suitable for working on a large and complex activity.
- General management and leadership skills appropriate to the size and seniority of the programme management team.

The requirements for a project manager are described in more detail on page 82. In addition to project management knowledge, the programme manager should have:

- A practical understanding of business value and benefits realisation.
- A practical understanding of change management and the ability to transition deliverables from the programme to business-as-usual operations.
- The ability to interact with and influence senior managers and executives.
- General management skills that would be associated with any senior manager.
- The leadership skills to direct a significant endeavour.
- Where appropriate, knowledge of programme management methodologies such as MSP (Managing Successful Programmes).
- An awareness of governance processes.
- The ability to drive structure and clarity in situations of ambiguity and uncertainty.

Often programme managers also need to have the capability to manage third-party vendors in the delivery of all, or some, projects within the programme.

Programme reporting

Reporting programme status is similar to reporting project status (see pages 107 and 110), but is more difficult because of the scale and complexity of a programme. Additional information that can be in a programme status report compared to a project report includes:

- Commentary on programme status.
- Summary of status by project.
- Status of dependencies between projects.
- Cross-programme risks, issues, changes, etc.
- Progress towards programme objectives or business benefits.

The needs of big projects or programmes

The checklist on page 60 listed the critical success factors (CSFs) for projects. These all hold true for programmes as well. However, on top of that there are additional CSFs for programmes and the largest of projects:

- Realistic planning horizons (generally, it is futile to commit plans for endeavours which have timeframes that are significantly longer than an organisation's strategic planning horizon).
- Effective governance processes in place.
- Acceptance of the needs for business change across the leadership of an organisation.
- Culture and management approaches which are supportive of benefits realisation.
- Senior management and executive-level support and leadership for the programme.

Portfolios and portfolio management

The terms *portfolio* and *portfolio management* are important in project management. There are various definitions of the words. The term *portfolio* is used as:

- An alternative word for programmes, especially those associated with a programme of work for a common customer, e.g. the sales portfolio.

- A set of projects which use the same resources to deliver, e.g. the new product development portfolio, or the IT portfolio.

- All the projects and programmes in an organisation, e.g. the XYZ Corporation's project portfolio.

- The governance processes used to align project delivery with business strategy, and those components of strategy to be delivered via projects, e.g. project selection and prioritisation.

In this book the term 'portfolio' encapsulates the last two definitions in the list.

Portfolio management involves selecting the right mix of projects to deliver the outcomes required by an organisation, taking account of resource limitations. Portfolio management has the following main tasks:

1   Determining portfolio objectives and metrics, e.g. what strategic or operational goals must be achieved in the next financial year(s) by projects; what balance of projects should be invested in?

2   Selecting projects in the portfolio, which is a form of investment decision making:

- Understand project options. Which projects can be considered for delivery? (See pages 53 to 57.)

- Understand constraints upon delivery and what resources are available. How many and what combinations of projects can be undertaken? (See page 191.)

- Understand and apply selection criteria, filter out or eliminate unsuitable projects and prioritise between those left. The intention is to match the projects undertaken to the resources available. (See page 189.)
- Review the complete set of projects in the portfolio and compare this to the portfolio objectives.

3   Managing the portfolio in-life, dynamically assessing and amending it (adding, deleting or changing projects, altering relative prioritisation of projects) as a result of:

- Project outcomes differing from plan, e.g. different resource usage, different time to deliver, different benefits stream.
- The operational situation changing, e.g. resources on projects are required in operations, or operational problems arising which require an unpredicted high-priority project to be delivered to overcome the problems.
- An unforeseen opportunity arising, e.g. an attractive sales opportunity which can only be fulfilled by a project.
- Business needs changing, e.g. alterations in competitive situation, or amendments to business strategy leading to the need to change the project line-up.

(Also see page 234.)

Portfolio reporting

Portfolio reports provide a view of the status of all projects in the portfolio, and a view of progress towards portfolio-level objectives. Portfolio reports are typically produced monthly or quarterly. Helpful contents are:

- Summary of status for projects and programmes in portfolio. For a complex portfolio the summary report for each project must be short. A useful format is a traffic light status (red–amber–green), with a commentary of 1–2 sentences per project.
- Cross-portfolio issues, e.g.:
    - Common issues and risks.
    - Common sources of change.
    - Resources shortages or issues coming up.
    - Any business issues with an impact on the portfolio.
- Modifications to the portfolio: new projects started, projects finished, projects on hold or stopped.
- Status of progress towards portfolio goals, i.e. how well the portfolio is progressing towards the delivery of strategic goals.
- Key decisions and approvals required relating to the portfolio.
- Portfolio commentary, e.g. a paragraph of information with summary comments on the portfolio status.

Choosing projects for a portfolio

Core activities in portfolio management are selecting and prioritising the projects an organisation will invest in. The way projects are prioritised depends on the portfolio objectives, which in turn depends on business strategy. Ways to prioritise projects include:

- Management judgement.
- Financial assessment, e.g. NPV or IRR.
- Impact on KPIs (Key Performance Indicators), how the projects will directly improve key business metrics.
- Strategic alignment, i.e. how the projects fit with business objectives as defined in the strategy.
- Feasibility, i.e. the likelihood of achieving the project, which includes technical, operational and commercial probability of success.
- Capability development, e.g. what learning opportunities a project provides to improve business capabilities and competencies.

A good way to prioritise between projects is to use multiple criteria based on business needs. The criteria should be scored and weighted for each project. Pure scoring is unlikely to be able to take account of the complexity and reality of business situations, and there is usually a need to apply management judgement as well. Having determined the approach to prioritisation the projects can be selected as follows:

1   Filter projects:
    - Remove projects which are culturally, socially or legally non-permissible.
    - Remove non-feasible projects, e.g. those which are not possible to complete, or not possible with the organisation's capability and an acceptable level of risk, or those projects which are operationally unacceptable.
    - Remove projects which do not meet minimum business case requirements or are outside other business thresholds, e.g. too long a payback period, above maximum scale.

2   Prioritise:

- Choose prioritisation criteria (as described above).
- Apply criteria by scoring each project against them.
- Prioritise projects.
- Compare prioritised list to resource available.
- Re-prioritise taking account of resource constraints.

3   Review:

- Check balance of projects. Is there a selection of projects that meets the needs of different stakeholder groups?
- Check against portfolio objectives. Will this set of projects deliver the business strategy?
- Check compatibility of projects. Are the projects compatible? For example, do any projects have conflicting goals, or can any projects be combined?
- Check cumulative risk. Does the portfolio have an acceptable level of risk, i.e. make sure some are low risk to balance against high-risk ones.
- Amend according to results of review.

4   Maintain portfolio over time with periodic reviews.

brilliant   tip

It is better to prioritise fewer projects and complete them than to start many projects and to spread resources so thinly that they take an extended period of time to complete, as the latter delays achievement of benefits.

Understanding human resource constraints and resolving conflicts

If there were no resource constraints, there would be no need for portfolio management, as any project with a positive business case could be delivered. To be able to decide how many projects should be done, it is important to be able to understand resource constraints.

There are various types of resources that have to be managed on a project:

- people
- money or budget
- equipment and facilities (non-consumables)
- consumables.

The focus in this checklist is on human resources, as these are complex to manage, and is the resource that typically provides the most contention on projects. There are several categories of human resources:

- Dedicated project professionals, such as project managers or business analysts, 100 per cent available for project work.
- Specialist resources who work predominantly on projects. For example, staff involved in new product development.
- People who are available for project work for a proportion of their time. An IT programmer may spend 50 per cent of his time on software development projects and 50 per cent on maintenance of existing systems.
- Operational people who are normally not available for project work, but who may be made available for specific projects.
- Contract staff, typically 100 per cent available once a contract is in place. (This requires permission to spend external budget.)

A project manager wants to ensure that sufficient resources exist to be able to complete the tasks on the project. From a portfolio level, human resources can be managed to achieve several different goals, e.g.:

- maximise flexibility and capability to respond to new opportunities
- maximise utilisation
- minimise staff costs
- maximise learning etc.

These are conflicting goals and it is important to understand which goal is paramount when dealing with resources. There are three ways to manage resource constraints:

- Resource limits – start new projects until no resource is available to do any more. This is simple, but usually inefficient and ineffective in maximising project returns.
- Detailed capacity analysis – understanding the availability of all resources in an organisation and managing access to those resources at a detailed level. This is theoretically best, but managing the detailed information to understand the availability and workload of all staff can be onerous.
- Availability tracking for key 'bottleneck' resources only – for example, only tracking availability of project managers. If the key bottleneck resource can be identified in an organisation – that is, the resource that usually constrains the ability to do more work – it is possible to effectively manage resources by controlling access to this subset of staff.

Without a project or programme team, a project/programme manager cannot deliver anything. Understanding what human resources are required, identifying resources, gaining commitment, keeping resources, and bringing new people in the team are critical tasks for project/ programme managers. Often the key project/programme management challenge is resource management.

At some point in almost every project there will be a conflict, when the same person or team of people will be required to do different tasks. This may be within a project/programme, or across projects within a portfolio.

There is no straightforward algorithm that will resolve all resource conflicts, but the following process can be applied:

1   Ensure projects are planned in advance to give maximum warning of resource bottlenecks. During planning apply resource levelling to try and remove bottlenecks.

2   Check if the resource constraint is real. Can additional resources be brought in to resolve the problem, e.g. from operational departments or by use of contractors?

3   Apply prioritisation criteria – ideally, the highest-priority project will gain first access to the resources required.

4   Determine if it is possible to reschedule one of the conflicting projects to a later date.

5   Factor in the duration that resources are required for by conflicting projects. For example, if a high-priority project requires a person for six months continually, and a lower-priority one requires the same person for one day, it can be effective to let the low-priority project continue by providing the person for one day even if the work is of lower priority. However, you cannot continually or even regularly do this or the first project will never be delivered.

brilliant   recap

Projects rarely exist in isolation. Programme and portfolio management provide the toolkit to select, prioritise and deliver multiple projects successfully and in line with an organisation's operational needs and strategy.

CHAPTER 12

Managing a project management team

Project management departments are an important function in many organisations. This chapter contains checklists for setting up and running a team of project managers.

The function and roles of the project management team

One way to provide the project managers and associated support staff in a business is to set up a project management team as part of the permanent organisational structure. The precise function of this team varies. Important functions of this team include:

- Recruiting sufficient project management resource to deliver prioritised projects.
- Providing access to additional project managers on a temporary or contract basis when the project workload is above normal.
- Delivering projects and programmes.
- Providing regular, reliable information on project status to provide up-to-date information and support decision making.
- Developing confidence in the organisation's ability to deliver projects, and supporting the wider management community in making business commitments based on project delivery.
- Developing relevant project management tools, techniques and processes.
- Building appropriate project management infrastructure (see page 210).
- Acting as the role model for best practice delivery of projects.
- Developing and enhancing an organisation's project management capability.
- Putting HR policies and performance management approaches in place to motivate project managers to continue to deliver successfully.

There are several roles that can exist within a project management team. The roles required depend upon the scale of the organisation, the type of projects it invests in, and the size of the project portfolio. The following table lists roles which may be part of this team. These are roles and not individuals. In some cases the role may be combined into part of a larger job, in other situations there may be several people with each of these roles.

Role title	Core responsibilities
Manager of project managers	Overall management and development of the project management team.
Resourcing manager	Allocating project managers to projects and for planning resource needs relative to the portfolio plans. (See pages 92, 97 and 191.)
Portfolio manager	Portfolio management, the development of the portfolio and interfacing portfolio management processes into governance processes. (See page 186.)
Project managers	Delivery of projects. (See page 82.) There may be a hierarchy of project managers based on skills and experience, e.g. junior and senior project managers.
Programme managers	Delivery of programmes, which may consist of several projects. (See page 183.) There may be a hierarchy of programme managers based on skills and experience, e.g. programme manager and programme director.
Project office staff	A variety of tasks supporting project and programme managers, and overall management of the team. (See page 207.)
Specialist project management support, e.g.:	Provide in-depth expertise to support project managers in aspects of projects and to provide advanced processes and tools. Also, can ensure common standards are adhered to.
Risk specialist	Provide specialist risk management support, e.g. quantitative assessment techniques.
Project planner	Provide specialist planning support.
Specialist roles which support projects, e.g.:	In-depth expertise to support the delivery of projects with skills that sit outside the scope of project management, but which are integral to successful delivery.

→

Role title	Core responsibilities
Business analyst	Provide business analysis expertise to be used in scoping projects and requirements analysis.
Change manager	Provide change management expertise to ensure that projects result in sustained change.
Benefits manager	Provide benefits management expertise to ensure that projects maximise benefits and meet business cases.

Sizing and structuring a project management team

There are several ways to structure a project management team:

- The team can be centralised with all project managers in one team, or distributed across an organisation:
  - Centralised: favours development of specialist expertise and facilitates better control by portfolio management, but risks being bureaucratic and unresponsive to operational needs.
  - Decentralised: a good way to get rapid response to project needs and for project managers to develop content knowledge, but makes it harder to ensure consistent quality of project management, to perform portfolio management and ensure most efficient allocation of resources to highest-priority projects.

Often a combined model is best with a central team of project managers responsible for complex cross-functional endeavours, and project managers distributed in the line functions responsible for departmental projects.

- Centralised teams can be organised by:
  - Customer or functional group: mapping project managers to the organisation structure, e.g. having project managers for sales, operations and the corporate functions. This enables project managers to develop expertise in the area of the business they support.
  - By skill set, e.g. IT project managers, business change project managers, performance improvement project managers. This enables project managers to develop expertise in the type of projects they support.
  - By account manager and resource manager: have account managers facing each of the key stakeholders responsible for managing customer relationships and staffing projects. The team can have separate resource managers responsible for line managing project managers.

Sizing a project management team can be difficult as the number and scale of projects fluctuates. Three basic ways to size the project management team are:

- Sizing based on the peak workload: building a project management team that can fulfil the maximum workload. This provides great flexibility, but can be at significant cost.

- Sizing based on the average volume of projects: a steady resource level capable of handling the typical volume of projects, and using contract or temporary resource for workload above this peak.

- Do the reverse. Don't size the project management team in relation to the number of projects – determine the volume of projects by the number of project managers. Use the project management team as a deliberate bottleneck, to limit the total number of projects started to those that this team can manage. Once all project managers are busy no further projects can be started until a project completes. This can be effective because:

  - There will always be a resource bottleneck in your organisation. By making it the project management team you can manage it, and you can ensure other teams do not become overloaded with work. A single resource bottleneck can be understood and controlled and the workload can be optimised.

  - It will happen anyway. If you try to staff to your peak project workload, you will find that project managers are *always* busy as there is a continuous appetite for projects.

Recruiting project managers

If you want to build a project management team you will have to recruit project managers. The steps in recruiting project managers are:

1   Start by being clear about the need – what specifically are you after?

- How many project managers? (See page 200.)
- What types? (See page 197.) Think through the range of projects you will have. Not every project needs a senior programme manager!
- What skills and experience do the project managers need beyond project management? (See pages 82, 94, 183 and 197.) For example:
  - Industry knowledge
  - Technical skills
  - Methodology knowledge
  - Other context or specialist capabilities
  - General management skills.
- What are the requirements for all employees, including cultural fit with your organisation? Discuss it with your HR department.
- Determine type of employment (see page 203):
  - Permanent
  - Contract
  - Temporary.

2   Determine sources of staff:

- Do staff need to have full experience or can they be trained and developed on the job?
- Should staff be existing employees, or will external recruitment take place?

3   Develop selection criteria and competency framework based on point 1.

4   Advertise roles.

5   Interview candidates, and recruit according to the defined selection criteria.

General tips for selecting project managers:

- Regard accreditation as useful, especially in more junior staff. But look for proven delivery experience as essential.
- Remember you are not recruiting for any projects. You want staff who can deliver projects in your organisation with its specific characteristics.

- When interviewing candidates ask them to run through examples of projects they have managed. It's easy to talk about the theory and how well things went, so to really test competence we must focus on talking about problem situations and how the candidates overcame them.
- Find out about *their* roles in past projects, not about the project or project team in general.
- Always go for quality candidates rather than the quantity of candidates you need.

You can choose to staff a project management team with employees or make use of contract or temporary staff. Factors to take into consideration when choosing between internal and contract project managers are listed in the following table:

Factors	This factor favours the use of . . .
Highly variable project workload.	Contract resources as the number of project managers can be altered as the workload varies.
High variability in type of project work performed, requiring specialist skills.	Contract resources as an organisation may not have the ability to employ a wide range of project managers with specialist skills.
Low variability in quantity and type of projects.	In-house project managers.
Organisations which value flexibility in cost base and the ability to rapidly reduce costs.	Contract resources, as contracts can be terminated at short notice.
Need to minimise costs in the organisation.	In-house resources as average cost is typically lower.
Learning required.	In-house resources – any learning done by contractors is lost as soon as projects complete.
The projects often deal with sensitive information, commercial secrets or intellectual property development.	In-house resources who remain with the company when a project is completed.
There is a tendency for outsourcing work in the organisation.	Supplier staff. (Where projects are outsourced, the outsourced suppliers usually provide project managers.)

Setting project management objectives

Project managers benefit from clear performance objectives, which annual appraisals can be based on. Suggested areas for consideration in setting project managers objectives:

- Project success objectives:
  - Delivery of projects to predicted time and budget, with consideration given to the complexity, risk and degree of change associated with the specific projects the project manager is responsible for.
  - Meeting project business case objectives.
  - Client satisfaction and expectations management, to be based on direct stakeholder feedback.
  - Fulfilling your project processes – e.g. compliance with regular reporting rules.
- Personal development:
  - Enhancement of knowledge of project or programme management, including achieving specific accreditation.
  - Enhancement of knowledge of related disciplines (e.g. change management, benefits management and business analysis).
  - Enhancement of knowledge required in role (e.g. technical or business skills).
- Cultural fit with organisation and team.
- Benefiting the wider organisation:
  - Development of organisation's project management methods and standards.
  - Supporting the development and coaching of other project managers with less experience.
- Organisational link: project manager objectives should be linked to wider organisational performance goals, e.g. – company profitability, etc.

Developing project management skills

The skills of project managers can be developed through the following steps:

1   Start with an understanding that each person is unique, learns in an individual way and has individual learning needs.

2   Set development goals as part of the regular appraisal process, where goals are continuously refined and progress towards them is reviewed.

3   Link development of skills to a definition of ideal skills or competency framework at the level the project manager is operating at, the skills needed to work at a more senior level, and the wider needs of the organisation.

4   Use a variety of ways to develop skills, including:

   • Formal training, which may or may not end in accreditation. If you use accreditation, remember that the accreditation should not be an end in itself – it indicates a level of competence. It is only of value if a project manager's performance improves once the accreditation is achieved.

   • Team meeting and informal discussion groups, sharing experience across projects. Teaching others is a great way to improve your own knowledge. Bring project managers together to review issues and problems and the ways they were overcome.

   • Self-research. There is a huge amount of literature and computer-based training available on project management.

   • Learning on the job. This does require a willingness to expose project managers to new situations and involve them constantly in different project management challenges.

   • Project reviews (see Chapter 9). Project reviews are a critical part of learning and skills development.

5   Manage the development process. Learning will occur whatever process is in place, but it will not be optimised unless it is managed. For example, if you want someone to learn on the job you have to put them into situations that provide the opportunity to develop the relevant knowledge.

Managing and motivating a project management team

For project managers to perform at their best they need to be managed and motivated to encourage a high performance. Project managers are more likely to be motivated if they work in an organisation which has:

- A culture that values the role of the project manager and sponsorship from one or more executives for the development of project management skills in the organisation.

- Clear role definitions for project managers.

- Performance metrics and general HR policies which assess performance and allow rewards in a way that is appropriate to project managers.

- A defined career path within the organisation, whether or not that is to continue to work in the project management family of jobs.

- A variety of interesting projects to work on.

- The availability of personal development. Formal training courses, pathways to accreditation, aligned with continuous professional development requirements of associations such as APM, mentoring, and exposure to varied projects.

- Realistic expectations of what can be achieved by project managers. It is good to have high expectations of project managers, but there should be realism as to what is and is not achievable within the environment and resources of a specific organisation.

- Rewards in line with market expectations for the type and scale of role performed.

- Good supporting processes and tools. (See page 210.)

The project management office

A *project management office* (PMO) is a valuable part of many project management teams. Project management offices have a variety of roles, and should be structured according to the situation. It may also be known as a *programme management office*, or simply a *project office*.

Typical responsibilities include one or more of the following:

- Administrative support to the project management team.
- Collecting and aggregating information from projects, such as weekly reports, time sheets and project resource requests.
- Developing and maintaining the project management infrastructure.
- Owning project management standards.
- Analysis of plans and other reports across projects to support cross-project issue, risk and dependency management.
- Document control, library management and knowledge management across the project management community.
- Provision of the specialist resources to be utilised when required, e.g.:
  - project planner
  - risk manager
  - benefits manager
  - portfolio manager.

To set up a PMO:

1 Determine who the customers of the PMO are. This could be one or more of:
   - management of project managers
   - project and programme managers
   - portfolio managers
   - other senior stakeholders across the organisation.
2 Determine needs of the customer(s).
3 Determine structure, size and location of PMO.
4 Gain budget and approval to set up PMO.
5 Recruit necessary staff to fulfil identified roles.
6 Put necessary tools and systems in place.

Choosing project management software and tools

There are many project management software tools. Many organisations buy software on a piecemeal basis, and end up with a hotchpotch of incompatible systems. Selecting software should be a managed process. Choosing, installing and achieving benefits from project management software is a project of moderate complexity in its own right.

The steps to select software are:

1 Determine who the stakeholders in the process of selecting software are and who is the decision maker or arbitrator. You need a small group of people who will work together to specify and select the software you need. You will also need a decision maker who has final say in what is selected and will arbitrate over any disputes.

2 Determine what you are trying to achieve. Are you buying tools to make your project managers more efficient, to provide better management information, or to overcome some project management weaknesses? (If it is the last, take care, software alone will not overcome that many problems.)

3 Determine what budget is available – this may effectively constrain your choices. Some of the sophisticated tools offer great functionality, but at a relatively high cost. At the other extreme are shareware packages.

4 Decide if you are primarily buying tools to fit your processes, or if you are willing to adapt your approach to fit the tools. Unless you develop the software yourself you are likely to have to amend your processes or approach when buying off-the-shelf packages.

5 Identify the 'must-haves'. For example, does the software tool have to fit with your overall project management approach? Do you use critical path or critical chain? Do you use a standard methodology such as Prince 2 or MSP?

6 Inform yourself: research what tools are available. There are specialist project management tools, professional services automation tools, and many ERP systems have project-management-related components for activities like project budgeting.

7 Develop a specification. What functionality do you need? Consider:

- Planning tools – single project.
- Planning tools for multiple projects, and to integrate plans.
- Resource management and time-sheet systems.
- Communication tools.
- Information sharing and databases.
- Programme management tools.
- Portfolio management tools.

8 Compare and select from the tools that are available.

- Try to understand how the different tools work, e.g. most planning tools offer resource levelling, but how do they do it, and is it right for you?
- If you need tools to integrate, make sure that they have the necessary interfaces and can share data in compatible formats.
- If you have the time and the opportunity, try to speak to other users of the tools and understand how good they are in practice.

9 Develop an implementation plan.

10 Determine the actual costs, make a business case, prepare a budget and approve the plan. (The price of the software will only be a fraction of overall implementation costs.)

11 Install and amend working approach: this is a project with a change management element. All project managers and related staff will need education and training.

12 Review implementation and overcome outstanding problems.

Project management infrastructure

An organisation must develop an infrastructure to support project managers. This infrastructure must be sized and scoped according to the needs of the organisation. Useful components to consider are:

- Project or programme management standards, processes, role definitions and a competency framework.

- Software tools to support areas such as planning, resource management, portfolio management, along with reporting tools with common access.

- Document templates, e.g. project scoping documents, business cases, feasibility studies.

- Governance and portfolio management processes.

- Knowledge capture and learning support tools.

- Document sharing and team working tools.

- Project manager or programme manager role and competency definitions, and associated training materials.

- Reference guides such as standard risk checklists.

- A library of project management books or ebooks and related subjects to refer to.

- Customer engagement model. Defining when customers can, should or must come to you for project management resource, and how they engage you.

brilliant   recap

An effective way to fulfil the constant demand for projects is to set up an adequately resourced project management team as a permanent part of a company's organisation. This should be supported with appropriate policies and a comprehensive project management infrastructure.

PART 4

Achieving results and realising benefits

Project managers and project team members tend to focus on the deliverables their project is meant to produce. An emphasis on the development of quality deliverables, to time and budget, is important. But projects don't just produce deliverables. The deliverables are created to support improvement, or more generally change, in an organisation. It is through this change that benefits are achieved. This part covers change management and benefits realisation.

There are two chapters in this part:

13 **Handover and change** – changing an organisation as a result of
a project.

14 **Achieving business value** – making sure any task achieves what it was meant to achieve.

CHAPTER 13

Handover and change

This chapter deals with the implementation and handover of project deliverables, and the resulting organisational change.

Introduction

This chapter deals with the implementation and handover of project deliverables, and the resulting organisational change. Creating quality deliverables is not enough; they have to be *used*. If the deliverables are not used, nothing changes once the project is complete. That means no benefits will be realised.

Change is an inevitable outcome of successful projects, but it should not be left to chance. Change can be managed through *change management*. Change management is a complex subject and this chapter introduces project managers to the subject.

The term *operations* is used as shorthand for the parts of the business that project deliverables are implemented in, and which change as a result of this implementation.

Preparing for project handover and operational readiness

Many projects complete by handing over deliverables to operations. Operations must take ongoing responsibility for the maintenance of the deliverables. There is a big difference between simply handing deliverables to operations (often called '*throwing them over the wall*') and performing an effective handover.

If you want your project to lead to sustained change, a well-managed handover is essential. Key steps in an effective handover are:

- Develop a handover plan. Be willing to adapt this plan to respond to unexpected situations. Handover is complex and should not be a one-line item in the project plan. Handover needs to be broken into its constituent tasks, with responsibility allocated for completing each task.
- Confirm that appropriate levels of testing and verification are completed before moving into handover.
- Check that the deliverables from the project are in an acceptable state, meeting the quality needs of the organisation.
- Resolve any major issues associated with the project or the deliverables.
- Confirm that operational departments are aware and ready for the handover – and ready for the process of changing as the handover occurs.
- Ensure that the operational departments are capable of handling the deliverables.
  - Assess what skills or knowledge is required to use the deliverables to their full potential.
  - Identify any capability gaps between what is required and the current capability of the organisation.
  - Close gaps by appropriate measures, e.g. training and education, recruitment of new staff, defining service-level agreements for support, or putting maintenance contracts in place. This should be completed as a planned part of the project.

- Ensure operations are willing to take responsibility and have the capability to resolve any minor issues that have not been fixed as part of the project.
- Understand the impact on operations during change and adapt performance measures appropriately for the period of change.
- Check that ongoing budgetary ownership is clear, and that there are sufficient funds allocated in the budget to take on responsibility for the deliverables.

Dealing with resistance and support

An aspect of any change is that some people will support it and others will resist it. Reacting to change is natural. If a change is to be sustained, support for the change must be greater than the resistance to it. Effective change management requires reactions to be assessed, and resistance and support dealt with. (Also see page 56.)

- Prepare for dealing with resistance and support, and ensure there is sufficient time and resource in the project plan to handle it.
- Identify a senior sponsor who is willing to drive the change and the need for the change. The sponsor must be willing to spend significant time convincing people of the need for the change.
- Identify which stakeholders are affected by the change. This is usually staff and teams in your organisation. If appropriate, consider groups external to your organisation (e.g. customers and suppliers).
- Determine the impact of the change upon each of the identified individuals and groups.
- Eliminate any stakeholder groups who are really peripheral from further consideration. You cannot manage everyone's response.
- Predict the response to the change from the remaining stakeholders.
- Determine planned actions to use the support and overcome resistance. Sometimes actions, to make use of support or overcome resistance, require you to adapt your project approach. Do this willingly, as overcoming resistance is a core component of any change project.
- Implement the identified actions.
- Monitor response to actions. Plan and implement subsequent actions. Continue to do this until the change is successful.

Tips for managing resistance and support:

- Accept that managing resistance and support is one of the main activities when dealing with a project that leads to significant change.
- Listen to resistance. Often resistance will be reasonable, and you may get some great ideas and want to change a project as a result of them.

- Don't assume that a supporter is in favour of every aspect of a change. For example, it is not unusual to find people who agree with the principle of change, but who do not agree with the way the change is being pursued.

- Don't assume that power and rational argument will overcome all resistance. Forcing people to change will lower their motivation and may make resistance become hidden, which is harder to deal with. Some resistance will be at an emotional level, and rational argument alone will not overcome it.

- When dealing with people's reactions you cannot fully predict the nature or strength of their response. Therefore, in any situation in which a response is likely you need to be willing to tailor your plan to handle it.

- Try to be open and communicate as much as possible. This is not always practical, but if you can keep your actions in line with your communications you will develop greater trust, which will make your job easier.

- Don't assume that just because you have said something once that anyone has heard or understood. Key messages need to be repeated many times, often in different ways.

Deciding when to go live

A change is a transition from one way of working to a new way of working. This transition period is known as *go-live*. Go-live should not happen just because a project ends, but needs to take into account a number of factors. There is usually no perfect time to go live, and a balance has to be found between the factors listed in the following table:

Factors to consider when selecting go-live times	Implications
What type of implementation approach is being used, and does this have implications for go-live?	If big bang: • Delay until as much testing and preparation as possible can be done. If phased or pilot implementation: • Initial go-live can be done more quickly with less rigorous testing (see pages 129 and 215).
Type of deliverables or changes and organisational familiarity with them	The more familiar changes – consistent with existing ways of working deliverables – are the quickest to implement and go-live can be done, as the risk is lower. Completely novel change should be done with more care.
How quickly the project resources need to be released (there is an opportunity cost of keeping resources for an extended period on any project)	The higher the opportunity cost of keeping resources on a project, the quicker the project should go live to release project team members (see page 136).
How quickly the benefits from the project are required	The more quickly benefits are required, the sooner the project should go live (see Chapter 14).
When the operational departments are ready	Go-live should be performed when operational departments are ready to handle the change without an unacceptable reduction in performance levels (see also pages 221 and 225).

→

Factors to consider when selecting go-live times	Implications
The impact of the change on the operational departments	The higher the impact, the more care needs to be taken with go-live.
The wider status of the operational departments, e.g. peak or lull in workload; what other changes are ongoing	Go-live should be coordinated with an operational department's workload. Make changes during lulls in workloads – not during peak times. Do not do too many changes in parallel – changes should be phased (see page 225).

Supporting the organisation during implementation

A key factor in successful change management is the level of support provided to the organisation beyond the immediate project. From the narrow perspective of creating quality deliverables such support is often unnecessary, but to ensure a successful and sustained change, it is usually essential.

Key tips:

- Communications are central to change – without adequate communication, effective change is unlikely.
  - Keep everyone informed of what is going on and what is planned.
  - Tailor communications to suit different audiences.
  - Be willing to communicate key messages repeatedly. It can take several attempts for people to grasp and accept some components of change.
- Make sure senior line managers understand the change, support it, and act in a way that is consistent with it.
- Listen to staff and provide a way for them to raise concerns and make suggestions.
  - Deal with all concerns. Even if it is only to say nothing can be done, explain why nothing can be done.
  - Be alert to suggestions and worries of staff directly impacted by the change.
- Try to involve people in the change. People are more likely to accept change if they feel involved in it.
- Ensure you are creating and implementing quality deliverables. If the deliverables are not good enough, don't go ahead with the implementation. Whatever the benefits of quickly finishing the project, there will be a high and long-term price for poor-quality deliverables.
- Keep everyone doing what they are meant to do during the implementation. An organisation cannot stop simply because a change is under way. Normal work has to continue, as far as possible, uninterrupted.

- Expect and plan for a dip in operational performance. Good change management minimises the depth of the dip in performance, and the length of time it goes on for, but it is inevitable. Expectations should be managed regarding anticipated performance declines during change.

- Help people adapt to the change, accepting that different people take different lengths of time to adapt and require different types of support.

- Expect the unexpected! Be ready to resolve unpredicted problems and respond to unexpected outcomes. Build some contingency into your plan to handle this. Implementation is the time when the most unexpected problems occur.

- Keep the project team on board. Thanking people goes a long way towards maintaining motivation. Ensure there are appropriate rewards and celebrations as the change completes – you will soon need the same people for the next project, so it's worth leaving them with a positive attitude.

Determining when a change is complete and if it is successful

Organisations are never static. They undergo a constant series of changes. It is not always clear when one change finishes and the next starts. Indications that a change is complete and successful are:

- The project that caused the change is complete and resources released.
- The deliverables are signed off and handed over.
- Focus is now on the future and the next change. The project or the problems it created are yesterday's news.
- The project deliverables are in productive use. Too many projects complete and at the end of them no one does anything differently. If no one in the organisation is doing anything differently – no change has occurred.
- Benefits are being realised.
- The change is sustained and has become the standard way of working. It is no longer regarded as a change.
- The organisation has learnt what it can from the process of changing.

Critical success factors for change

There are many factors which contribute to the success of change. Some of the most important factors that lead to successful changes are:

- The change has a clear direction that is relevant and widely understood.
- There is an accepted need for change and an associated sense of urgency to change.
- There is a consensus that the particular change being pursued is a good way to achieve the outcome desired.
- Active, visible leadership and sponsorship for the change exists at a sufficiently senior level. The behaviour of senior managers and executives is consistent with change.
- HR policies and the performance management system are consistent with the change, and people are rewarded for acting in a way that is in harmony with and reinforces the change.
- There are adequate communications, and staff feel they have been kept informed.
- The project team driving the change, and the change sponsor, listen to the organisation. People perceive they are listened to with understanding and their concerns are dealt with.
- The project team are focused on the *change*, not simply the creation of deliverables or completing the tasks in the plan. This includes the human dimension as well as the technical dimensions of the project.
- The change is managed in a flexible way. There is a plan, but it is understood that the change won't happen exactly as planned. There will be unexpected outcomes and they must be managed.
- The organisation feels involved in the change and has the capacity (resources, time and emotional capacity) to deal with the change.
- Project and business impact risk are continually assessed and managed as the change progresses.

Managing multiple changes in parallel

In many organisations a significant challenge is delivering an ongoing series of changes successfully. Factors to consider are:

- Ensuring that the different changes are consistent and complementary, e.g. there is little point in running a project to improve staff morale at the same time as a headcount reduction project.

- Implementing the different changes in the most efficient way. For example, can some changes be combined into a single project without making the project excessively complex or risky?

- The experience of the organisation and the impacted operational departments in handling change. Organisations in which change is common develop expertise in handling changes. Care should be taken in organisations which are unfamiliar with change, and implementing too ambitious a change too quickly should be avoided.

- Variations in the operational departments' capacity and capability to accept and absorb the change. Human beings can only cope with so much change at any one time. Changes need to be planned from the viewpoint of the departments being changed, taking account of:

    - Operational impact of the change. An organisation can normally accept a maximum decline in performance at any one time. Too many changes at once will have an overly detrimental impact on performance.

    - Human resources allocated to the change project. Every change project needs people. Do too many projects at once and there will not be enough staff to perform business-as-usual operations.

    - The complexity of the change. People take time to understand and learn how to work in a changed way. Perform too many changes at once, and staff will struggle to cope.

brilliant recap

All projects result in change. If there is no change, the project has delivered nothing. Change management is an important supporting pillar to most business projects.

CHAPTER 14

Achieving business value

This chapter contains checklists to help projects or programmes achieve their planned benefits. The name for this approach is *benefits management* or *benefits realisation*. Benefits management is an essential part of any business project. If you cannot measure the benefits achieved, you cannot be sure that the project investment was worthwhile. This chapter also includes checklists to link projects with budgets and organisational strategy.

Identifying benefits

The starting point for achieving value from a project is to identify the benefits it will deliver.

- Benefits are identified during business case development. Benefits should be aligned with the business strategy, e.g. if the strategy is to be a low-cost business, then cost reduction benefits are of paramount importance (see page 237).
- There are several categories of possible benefit types:
  - Financial, e.g. cost reduction, cost avoidance, revenue increase.
  - Tangible and measurable, e.g. customer advocacy increase, staff satisfaction increase, changes in operational KPIs (Key Performance Indicators). Some of these may be convertible to financial measures if desired; for instance, an operational performance improvement can usually be converted to a cost saving or revenue increase.
  - Intangible and immeasurable, except by subjective judgement, e.g. strategic alignment, capability improvement, skills development.
- Project benefits should be subject to change control as the project progresses. Rarely will actual benefits match those expected when the project started.
- Expected levels of benefits to be achieved should factor in the risk associated with a project. No one should commit to delivery of 100 per cent of benefits from high-risk projects. However, across a portfolio of projects it is reasonable to expect 100 per cent of planned benefits to be achieved.

Tips for achieving identified benefits:

- Design projects to deliver benefits. Don't work out benefits when you have an idea for a project: select projects which will achieve the benefits desired. If you need cost reductions, identify cost-reduction projects; if you need revenue increases, identify revenue-increasing projects, etc.
- Plan projects to maximise benefits. Projects are often planned with a focus on deliverable creation and resource usage without considering benefits.

Project managers should constantly be looking for ways to maximise the benefits a project delivers. The way a project is managed will impact the speed and level of benefits.

● Take care when mixing benefit types. Different types of benefits can conflict from a change management perspective, and may also clash in terms of project strategy, e.g. cost reduction and customer service improvement benefits may require different project strategies.

● Check that the project is really the source of the benefits. If the benefits can be achieved without the project, then the project is not beneficial. Often projects are started which claim to deliver benefits that are achievable without the project.

● Identify and avoid double-counting, i.e. claiming exactly the same benefit from two projects.

● Don't focus too much on financial benefits. Financial benefits are important, but don't become fixated on them, as there are also valuable non-financial benefits. A focus on financial returns alone can lead to an unbalanced portfolio.

Measuring and tracking benefits

Benefits need to be tracked and measured if you want value to be achieved. For many projects, benefits tracking takes place after the project is complete, when deliverables have been implemented. For some programmes, with phases of implementation, benefits will be achieved throughout the life of the programme and should be tracked as the programme proceeds.

When benefits are not tracked, they tend to disappear. Without tracking benefits, it is impossible to make an objective judgement of whether or not a project has been a success. By tracking benefits it is possible to reward staff for achievements, and so motivate them for future projects.

The steps in measuring and tracking benefits are:

1   Start by being sure that you know what the expected benefits will be.

2   Understand what direct or indirect data are required to measure achievement of the benefit.

3   Have a mechanism to collect the data related to benefits and report on it in a structured format.

   - This may require activity in the project to put the processes in place if the data are not already collected in the organisation.

   - Baseline data are also required. A benefit is shown by a change in a measure, not by an absolute amount. Measuring a business's costs at £1 million per annum after a project tells you nothing. If baseline costs were £1.1 million before the project, costs have declined by £100,000.

4   Assign responsibility for measurement. Someone needs to be assigned with responsibility for collecting and assessing data. Be prepared for the fact that the measurement may have to go on for months, or even years, after delivery.

Additional tips for measuring and tracking benefits:

- Remember that just because a metric changes does not mean that a specific project caused it to change. There must be a causal link.
- Some important benefits will be intangible. Just because they are intangible does not mean that measurement should be abandoned. Intangibles can be indirectly measured by assessing opinions. Although this is subjective, it may be worth doing.
- It is not possible to measure some types of benefits. If this is the case, agree this up front, rather than wasting energy trying to prove the unprovable.

Realising project benefits

Benefits are only achieved if something has changed. Achieving benefits is often known in business as *realising benefits*. Benefits are more likely to be realised when you:

1   Identify who is responsible for delivering the benefits. In many cases this will not be a member of the project team, but will be an operational manager in the organisation.

2   Gain acceptance up front from the responsible party that he is accountable for benefits realisation. This is a fundamental step both in successful change management and in achieving benefits. Without such agreement up front, it is very hard to deliver benefits.

3   Agree at the outset how and in what form the benefits will be delivered, e.g.:

   ● If a project reduces cost – are the benefits realised as cost savings or cost avoidance?

   ● If a project makes an organisation more efficient – are the benefits realised as headcount reductions or volume increases?

   ● If a project reduces expenditure – will the benefits lead to a budget reduction or funds available for other expenditures?

   ● Are the benefits incremental to budget, or are they already built into the budget?

4   Manage benefits expectations in line with any changes to the project. If the project is amended or modified in any way, the benefits may need to be updated.

5   Deliver the project, and assess the possible benefits again. Has the project delivered what it set out to do? Is it reasonable to expect the benefits to be delivered? There is no point trying to force delivery of benefits if a project has failed – but if you can, the project was unnecessary anyway!

6   Measure the delivery of benefits over time (see page 231).

7   Make the necessary changes in forecasts, budgets, headcount, performance targets, etc. as projects deliver. (If nothing changes, what has been delivered?)

8   If appropriate, seek proof, e.g. which budget has changed, which performance measure has improved.

Realising benefits across a portfolio

From a portfolio management perspective, the benefits delivered from an individual project are less relevant than the total benefits from all projects in the business. There can be a conflict between the needs of an individual project and the total benefits to the business from its investment in projects. Dealing with such conflicts is part of the challenge of portfolio management.

Considerations for benefits management from a portfolio perspective are:

- Project prioritisation should reflect benefits.
- Portfolio management should ensure the delivery of a balanced range of different types of benefits.
- An individual benefit can only be delivered once. By looking across the whole project portfolio and by knowing everything that is going on, double-counting should be reduced, with each benefit assigned to one project only.
- Portfolio management should perform a sanity check across projects, e.g. if two projects separately claim to increase a performance metric by 10 per cent, do you really believe it will go up by 20 per cent if you do both projects? It is common to find that when the benefits from all the projects are totalled they add up to infeasible amounts.
- Project activity should be phased to maximise benefits and speed benefits. You want to maximise the returns from projects in the minimum amount of time. This is rarely achieved by starting as many projects as possible.
- Portfolio management should ensure that projects which are not delivering, or which have changed to such an extent that the benefits are lower than the cost to deliver, are stopped.
- The selection of projects should be changed as predicted benefits change.
- It is essential to take account of risk in assessing cumulative benefits.
- Take advantage across the portfolio of the opportunity to balance high-risk projects with low-risk ones.

Linking projects to budgets

A project is an investment and it has to be budgeted for. Budgeting for projects is a continuous process that goes through the following stages:

1   Budget planning in Year 1:

- Set targets and goals for the following year (i.e. in Year 1 set targets and goals for Year 2, etc.). These may be performance targets, opportunities to take, problems to overcome, mandatory objectives, such as meeting regulatory goals, or strategic objectives.

- Identify projects that will meet these targets.

- Estimate expenditures to deliver projects in the following year, e.g.:

  - New projects contributing to next year's targets and goals.

  - Projects planned or expected to continue in the next year.

- Estimate benefits and costs to be realised from completed projects in the following year.

- Create an initial budget. To do this, you need to understand if you are doing zero-based budgeting (unusual), or last year's budget plus or minus some percentage for growth or cost reduction.

- Manage expectations and avoid surprises which may result in an absolute rejection of project ideas, especially if the budget you have created is significantly different from historic budgets.

- Undertake budgetary review and approval. There are usually several iterations of budgetary review. Each iteration typically requires amendments to proposed budgets to meet targets set by the executives of the organisation. Typical amendments include:

  - Reducing the costs of projects by removing projects the organisation cannot afford or reducing the scope of projects.

  - Modifying the project line-up to meet performance and strategic objectives not met by the originally proposed projects.

  - Adding unexpected expenditures on projects. This is common when departmental budgets are brought together into an overall business budget. Different departments make assumptions about what project costs other departments are bearing, which are often wrong. Although this can lead to identifying savings by removing projects which are budgeted for twice, it more often leads to additional costs for projects that have been missed.

- Changes to the expected benefits and costs from projects once they have been delivered.

- Finalise the budget for the following year.

- At the end of the current year:

  - Agree accruals to carry forward (if allowed under your company's accounting policy).

  - Identify any projects that are unexpectedly late and which will continue to require expenditure in the following year.

  - Identify and agree any expenditure which can be brought forward from the following year into the current one, and so reduce next year's budget.

2   Manage the budget in Year 2:

- Start new projects and continue projects from the previous year.

- Amend project expectations in line with project budget variances:

  - New unplanned projects: if new projects arise, this requires either additional budget or reducing the budget assigned for existing projects.

  - Deal with project cost overruns or under-spends. Overruns and under-spends may allow more or fewer projects to be undertaken (or have an impact on other areas of expenditure, such as operational costs).

- Amend actual budgets in line with benefits realisation variances.

- Start budget planning for Year 3.

Aligning projects with strategy

Most organisations have a strategy. It may be a formal and structured document, or it may be an informal and general statement of direction. The strategy should control the allocation of resources and influence which projects are chosen. Projects are one of the key ways of achieving strategy and should be aligned with it.

Important considerations in aligning projects with strategy are:

- Does your organisation have a clear strategy?
- Is it communicated and understood by project managers and project sponsors?
- Is the understanding in line with the latest version of the strategy and updated whenever the strategy evolves? How does this happen – and is it effective?
- Is the strategy considered when making project-related decisions and approvals?
- Are any of the projects mandatory, irrespective of strategy, e.g. legal and regulatory requirements?
- Do the remaining projects contribute to meeting strategic goals?
- Are the projects being run in a way that contributes towards achieving the strategy?
  - At a macro level, are project objectives aligned with strategy? For example:
    - Will the complete set of projects deliver the strategy desired?
    - Does each individual project move the organisation closer to its strategic goals?
  - At a micro level, are the daily decisions and choices being made consistent with strategy? For example:
    - Requirements selection: are requirements prioritised based on their conformance with strategy?
    - Time–cost–quality: is the balance between time, cost and quality consistent with the direction of the business?

brilliant   recap

Benefits should be the primary consideration when designing and delivering a project – not an afterthought to justify the investment. Projects can be managed to optimise the delivery of benefits; benefits tracking and realisation provides a way to do this. Unless benefits will be achieved, there is no reason to invest in a project.